or none at all!

TITANIC

Cecilia Corrigan

&NOW Books
Lake Forest College
2014

First published 2014 by &NOW Books, an imprint of
Lake Forest College Press.

Carnegie Hall
Lake Forest College
555 N. Sheridan Road
Lake Forest, IL 60045

lakeforest.edu/andnow

Lake Forest College Press publishes in the broad spaces of Chicago
studies. Our imprint, &NOW Books, publishes innovative and
conceptual literature and serves as the publishing arm of the
&NOW writers' conference and organization.

ISBN: 978-1-941423-99-8

Cover design by Emma O'Hagan

Cover image, *Courtesy Hiss*, Will Rahilly, 2013

Book design by Nura Husseini

Printed in the United States

LAKE FOREST
COLLEGE

BOOKS

Thank you to all those who supported this work, in particular Lisa Robertson, Madeleine Plonsker, and everyone at &NOW Books.

—Cecilia Corrigan

INTRODUCTION

In her submission note for her manuscript *Titanic*, Cecilia Corrigan spoke of her desire in this work to explore the cultural and syntactic tension experienced when "straddling worlds." Her reference was to the worlds of philosophy and poetry, or perhaps the worlds of poetry and television. As well as studying poetry and poetics at the University of Pennsylvania, she has studied philosophy, and has worked as a screenwriter for HBO. From my place as a reader—secluded, rural, and solitary—reading this wild text of Cecilia's inserted extra screens, jittery and scathingly brilliant and very funny, into my readerly cognition. She reminded me that indeed it is a world of screens now, even or especially off at the edge of things—the screens of our communications devices of course, such as this one, where I am writing now, the screens of the entertainment media that slide with such phantom immediacy into our affective lives and our memories, permeable decorative surfaces that obscure as they animate what they shelter, and the presciently named screen memories of Dr. Freud, where images, events, fantasies and errors combine to produce the wildly variable and shifting synthetic representations we call memory. In the screen structure, in the *Titanic*, representation and subjectivity are straddled by the erotics of a joyous doubt. Across this shimmery, sensing, and at times brutal tissue, a nomadic value animates not the referent, but the screen, not meaning but the covert passage of submorphemics, not signs but the dreams of diphthongs, not grammar but the livid Dante-esque reinvention of syntax as vernacular emotion, not the leveling of inflection but the embellishment of the caesura, not margins but markets inverted, not Lena Dunham's bad sex but Wittgenstein's bad romance. Because I was curious, because I like these things-- caesura, romance, vernaculars, submorphemics—I kept rereading. How does it work, is what I was asking.

Rhythm is key. But in *Titanic* rhythm is not the same as meter or regulating count. Like the linguist Emile Benveniste's critical reconfiguration of the atomist origins of the word *ruthmos*, rhythm here is a volatile improvisation glimpsed in passing as it ripples or scrunches across a body, a screen, a text, a desire in movement. Rhythm is disposition. Staccato as a social media feed, her prosody's plundered by emoticons, jump-cut, feedback, ghosts, full-bleed, jet-lag, Baroque elision. What we get is late capital's vernacular, the vulgar tongue of target markets exploded. If the effect is comedic, it is because our happiness might crave this parody of capital's time as disposition. Here we have the opportunity to glimpse our own lives as parodies of mass representation, instead of the inverse. The screen is the memory that precedes us. Unoriginal always, subjectivity agitates the propriety of products, striates representational superstructures.

I am very pleased to have landed in Cecilia Corrigan's neo-Kantian aesthetic of striving Hollywood losers where weird is the new sublime. For now to win is to lose everything, to sink while serenading endings, and a book is not a refuge but a rhythm generator for which there is no difference at all between the social and the subjective. So down with the coral reefs and the lampreys and the boulevards, let's be ghosts, let's name-drop and cruise, let's be, with comedic indiscretion, lyricists, Cecilia.

—Lisa Robertson

So imagine there's a dialogue
rooted in the fact that one guy has
a gun, and the point of the scene is
the other guy trying to get the gun
from the first guy. Now, replace the
gun with subjectively exclusive
epistemological understanding, and
you've got this scene we're working
on now.

—David Milch

Welcome me, if you will,
as the ambassador of a hatred
who knows its cause
and does not envy you your whim
of ending him.

—Frank O'Hara,
"For James Dean"

I was never very confident in my voice, you see.

So I thought, rather than just sing them which would probably bore the pants off everybody, I would uhm, I'd like to kind of *portray* the songs.

In rendering the book for you the somewhat unusual course has been adopted of printing the original side by side with the translation. Such a method of presentation seemed desirable both on account of the obvious difficulties raised by the vocabulary and in view of the peculiar literary character of the whole. As a result, a certain latitude has been possible in passages to which objection might otherwise be taken as over-literal.

This is a book for people who are interested in getting involved with the real world. If that doesn't suit you well, the doors right back where you came in.

No ?

Before we get started I'd like to tell you a little bit about me and where I'm "at" right now in my life. First off, I'm just come out and say that for about eight years now I've been a daily user of a .05 microgram compound of (S)-2-amino-3-[4-(4-hydroxy-3,5-diiodophenoxyl)-3,5-diiodophenyl] propanoic acid, which is being metabolized as we speak in my liver, kidneys, brain and muscles.

A game is an activity defined by rules in which players try to reach some sort of goal. Games can be whimsical and playful, or highly serious. They can be played alone or in complex social scenarios. Think about all the games you know you guys. Who did you play them with? That's right: your family!

Wait. Ok. I know I'm avoiding the topic. I also use, more or less every day, 0.15 mg of levonorgestrel, (d(-)-13 beta-ethyl-17-alpha-ethinyl-17-beta-hydroxygon-4-en-3-one), a totally synthetic progestogen, and 0.03 mg of ethinyl estradiol, (19-nor-17α-pregna-1,3,5 (10)-trien-20-yne-3,17-diol), cellulose,

9

D&C Red 30, FD&C Yellow 6, lactose, magnesium stearate, and polacrilin potassium to suppress my gonadotropins, inhibit my ovulation, thicken my cervical mucus and change my endometrium.

Now, about 27 years and 35 weeks ago, the development of my external genitalia would have been fully differentiated in my mom's uterus. My genitals would have started forming weeks before that. Now, let's say instead of the tiny cells of my clitoris and labia majora, a little penis had formed on me, around week 11 of my mom's pregnancy in the spring of 1986.

In this case I'd be a male baby, a man now. Let's call me David. Let's say I was taking a similar compound of synthetic estrogen, like maybe an extremely high dosage daily injection of stilboestrol. I'd experience a reduction in libido, reduced testicular size, impotence, and probably I'd begin to grow breasts and put on weight. It's likely I'd become depressed due to my hormonal imbalance, and become extremely lethargic, as the lack of testosterone would affect my mental acuity.

Before the symptoms became too brutal, I'd carry on with my television show, up until my first birthday in October 1987.

My television show has a live audience. They're responsive, engaged, and affectionate. Occasionally one of them will come up to me after the show, explain they have a fatal disease of some kind, say how much my show has helped them. We'll hug and I'll give them some merch. Sometimes I wonder what else I could have done, till I remember the substantial yearly donations to various "Cure for" charities.

I'm gonna tell you a love story.

CECILIA
Thank you! Th-thanks, thank you. Thank

you very much, good evening welcome
to the program! I'm your host Cecilia
Corrigan, there's this guy, what's his name
again, it's your musical host Paul Shaffer.

PAUL

Cecilia nice to see you.

CECILIA

Paul, did you see the TV movie the
Renee Richards story?

PAUL

I didn't catch the Renee Richards story.

CECILIA

(To audience)

What was that movie called, that Renee
Richards movie? Second Serve? Second
Serve all about Renee Richards who was
a -

PAUL

—Second Wha?

CECILIA

Second serve, a professional tennis player
who formerly was a man, an opt, uh
thamolic, uh surgeon an eye surgeon,
yeah—

PAUL

—Yeah, yeah—

CECILIA

—and uh then became female and played tennis for a number of years. You know I found, the most interesting thing was, the hardest part about becoming a woman for ah, Dr. Richards, was learning to like Tom Jones so- !

PAUL

(cracks up, claps, then playfully boos)

CECILIA

Aw stop it c'mon, hey! I'm just a kid trying to make a living, leave me alone, will ya! Uh.. what else, oh! this is exciting, the Pope is coming to visit the United States in the spring of 1987 he's going to visit Florida, he's gonna visit Texas, and he's also going to visit California and the purpose of his visit, he says, is to find the best damn chili dog in the united states.

Laughter

Also, Soviet dissident Anatole Shiranski met with Ronald Reagan yesterday and he asked him for- the president- and he asked him for his help getting Jews out of the Soviet Union. And, oddly enough this

morning, Ronald Reagan also got a call
from Kurt Waldheim asking for his help
in getting the jews out of Austria, so, it's
a very-

Laughter/Boos

CECILIA
(Nodding)

 are you fans of Kurt Waldheim, is that it?
Uh... What are we doin'? Oh what a show
folks Trisha Low is here, Marv Albert
is here, and another edition of stupid
pet tricks. Here we go again folks here's
what's his name, here's Paul.

PAUL
Thanks, thank you, etc. Long night ahead,
Cecilia?

CECILIA
No! does it, does it seem like it's gonna be
a long night? What are we doin' first, hate
mail?

PAUL
Yeah hate mail.

CECILIA
Ok. Let's see here.

Opens a letter from a viewer, reads

"Your discovery of the contradiction
caused me the greatest surprise and, I
would almost say, consternation, since
it has shaken the basis on which I
intended to build arithmetic.... It is all
the more serious since, with the loss of
my Rule V, not only the foundations of
my arithmetic, but also the sole possible
foundations of arithmetic, seem to
vanish."

"For English, press one. Para Espanol, oprima el dos. Pour le français, appuyez trois. Für Deutsch, Drücken Sie viermal."

Beep

"You have selected English. Welcome to the Guggenheim Museum. Thank you for joining us for our Spring 2003 exhibition season. If at any time you wish to hear a section repeated, just click the back button on your audio device. You can also skip to the next section by clicking the forward button.

"The Guggenheim Museum is at once a vital cultural center, an educational institution, and the heart of an international network of museums. Visitors can experience special exhibitions of modern and contemporary art, lectures by artists and critics, performances and film screenings, classes for teens and adults, and daily tours of the galleries led by experienced docents. Founded on a collection of early modern masterpieces, the Guggenheim Museum today is an ever-growing institution devoted to the art of the 20th century and beyond.

"Please select from the following exhibit features: Press one for an introduction to The Cremaster Cycle. Press two for Matthew Barney's Cremaster sculptures. Press three for Matthew Barney's Cremaster photographs. Press four for—"

Beep

"Matthew Barney's Cremaster Cycle sculptures share a common link in that they are derived from the multi-layered narratives of the project as a whole. The sculptures on view here are constructed from the artist's signature materials, including plastic, metal, and Vaseline. These sculptures function as three-dimensional incarnations of the characters and settings. They exist independently from the films, but embody the same content—now expressed in space rather than time. The sculptures you'll see here are largely sourced from the third film in the cycle, combined with works from the other parts of The Cremaster Cycle. The sculptures are displayed on the museum's ramp, paced in alignment with their order according to the cycle itself.

"To hear information about specific sculptures in the show, enter the first four letters of the sculpture's title."

Beep beep beep beep.

"You have selected *The Ehric Weiss Suite*. This piece, constructed with black acrylic, stainless steel, Vaseline, and live pigeon, is located on the museum's fifth floor, in a small room adjacent to the main gallery, visible through a transparent door. Truly one of the most melancholic and affecting works in the exhibit, the piece is constructed as a tribute to the death of Erich Weiss. The pigeons included in the installation are professionally rented from a carrier pigeon stable in Queens, New York. You'll notice that the coffin and the floor are encrusted with the shit of the pigeons and their feed. This is because they are there all the time. They are wearing black coats, because they are in mourning for Harry Houdini. Take care to stand clear of the unsealing door, please.

"Thank you. Please enter the installation through the now-opened Plexiglass door. The pigeons are well-trained and friendly. Simply remove your shoes if you are concerned about the ruination of their high quality due to the artwork's materials, i.e. pigeon guano. Please approach the coffin with care in order to affect a minimal amount of physical influence on the installation's composition, and on the psychological state of the pigeons.

"Stand aside for the opening coffin. Thank you. If you have any extra materials such as purses or sketchpads, please place them on the ground next to the coffin. Thank you. Please step up into the coffin to enjoy the full virtual reality design of the installation.

"Please step into the coffin.

"Please step into the coffin. Thank you. Please mount the Plexiglass and acrylic headset over your forehead with the viewing screen positioned to encompass your entire line of vision. Press four once you have mounted the headset.

"Press four once you have mounted the headset.

"Press four once y—"

Beep

"Thank you. Please lie back in the sculpture to begin the presentation.

Please lie back.

Please lie back in the—

I don't see why our story shouldn't be told, why our love is less valuable just because all statements on this page are false. Even though I had to let you sink into RL death, our love was as big and hard as any vanilla human on humans'. After all, isn't what everyone really wants an oceanic experience of complete integration with the Other? Isn't that where most of the brutality associated with love comes out, when we realize that there is a fundamental division between our cognitive realities which will never allow for a fully shared experience? Life is a bitch, death is her sister, sleep is the cousin, what a fuckin' family picture. You are as jaunty as a beetle. I love how we never fight now that you're gone, and never did when you were. Not only did you have an infinite knowledge of my cognitive processes, but you probably understand them better than I do my own text start to wait. You know Father Time, we all know Mother Nature. It's all in the family, but I am of no relation.

Ok so

I'll say I'm sleeping at Alice G's house,

And Alice, you can say you're sleeping at Henry's house,

Henry, say you're sleeping at Alan's house,

Alan, say you're sleeping at Ada's house,

Ada, say you're sleeping at Ludwig's house,

Ludwig say you're sleeping at Dawn's house,

Dawn, say you're sleeping at Christopher's house,

Christopher, say you're sleeping at Snow White's house,

Snow White, say you're sleeping at Elsa's house,

Elsa, say you're sleeping at Spike's house,

Spike, say you're sleeping at Leo's house,

Leo, say you're sleeping at Alice J's house,

Alice J, say you're sleeping at Norman's house,

Norman, say you're sleeping at Tim's house,

Tim, say you're sleeping at Graham's house,

Graham, say you're sleeping at Frank's house,

Frank, say you're sleeping at Mom's house,

Mom, say you're sleeping at Anna's house,

Anna, say you're sleeping at William J's house,

William J, say you're sleeping at William R's house,

William R, say you're sleeping at Selena's house,

Selena, say you're sleeping at Julianne's house,

Julianne, say you're sleeping at Willow's house,

Willow, say you're sleeping at Faust's house,

Faust, say you're sleeping at Lil Wayne's house,

Lil Wayne, say you're sleeping at Marshall's house

Marshall, say you're sleeping at Pepi's house,

Pepi, say you're sleeping at Mac's house,

Mac, say you're sleeping at Starbuck's house,

Starbuck, say you're sleeping at Paul's house,

Paul, say you're sleeping at Matthew's house,

Matthew, say you're sleeping at Pauline's house,

Pauline, say you're sleeping at Dan's house,

Dan, say you're sleeping at Siri's house,

Siri, say you're sleeping at David P's house,

David P, say you're sleeping at George's house,

George, say you're sleeping at Helo's house,

Helo, say you're sleeping at Hugo's house,

Hugo, say you're sleeping at Joan's house,

Joan, say you're sleeping at David M's house,

David M, say you're sleeping at Veronica's house,

Veronica, say you're sleeping at Katy's house,

Katy, say you're sleeping at Bertrand's house,

Bertrand, say you're sleeping at Anya's place,

Anya, say you're sleeping at Peli's place,

Peli, say you're sleeping at Virginia's place,

Virginia, say you're sleeping at John T's place,

John T, say you're sleeping at Faith's place,

Faith, say you're sleeping at Wilky's place,

Wilky, say you're sleeping at Christopher's Mom's place,

Christopher's Mom, say you're sleeping at Gottlob's place,

Gottlob, say you're sleeping at Cecilia's place,

Cecilia, say you're sleeping at Xander's place,

Xander, say you're sleeping at Sir Andrew Clark's place,

Sir Andrew Clark, say you're sleeping at Jos' place,

Jos, say you're sleeping at the Wicked Queen's place,

Wicked Queen, say you're sleeping at Giles' place,

Giles, say you're sleeping at Bob's place,

Bob, say you're sleeping at John M.K.'s place,

John M.K., say you're sleeping at Buffy's place,

Buffy, say you're sleeping at Nicholas' place,

Nicholas, say you're sleeping at Philip's place,

Philip say you're sleeping at Trisha's place,

Trisha, say you're sleeping at Dr. Baldwin's place,

Dr. Baldwin, say you're sleeping at my place,

And by the time they sort it out we'll be somewhere they'll never catch us.

This one mad pale girl used to have big sleepovers. I was invited at first, till I lied about having had a boyfriend the summer I'd lived in France. What gave me away was that I said he had a motorcycle: I was only 11! *Wight* is a word that

Sweetheart, you know what you are.

Sweetheart, your cock what it is.

When we met I was approximately fifty years old and you were approximately twenty-seven. I was a good teacher but sometimes I got in trouble for hitting the children. I'm talking about you because you were a different kind of smart than I was, but a kind I could still recognize as smart, which wasn't so common for me. I used to love giving you a hard time in my lectures, which were really more like debates, conversations between the two of us. I really went after you not like that—You see, I'd conflated you with my first love, an adolescent named Pepi who was our (double check) gardener's son. When my colleagues at Princeton University constructed the theater of computation, the universal machine, they allotted jobs to the various women "computers" with care, these are actual jobs you should be so lucky to get, in this economy, with these reparations, no, wait, wait,
wait
wait
wait
wait
wait
if

wait Waigt, wit Witt Weight wait, wait wigt wight, my wight, mye my only wight my wight wight wight wight wight please, don't don't leave me here, how much money do you need—

22

THE SUMMER I FELL IN LOVE WITH THE YOUNG PEPI IN THE BACKYARD AND HOW IT INFORMED MY PHILOSOPHY OF LANGUAGE

Isn't it terrible how lonely I am?
My Pepi I pretended to know your name
A true heart doesn't know who is murmuring,
Picture me murmuring.
My bad spelling in youth is connected with the whole
rest of my character.
I want to do everything to it, never have I ever been a margin
when I smoke no smoke comes out
When I love language, no whoa comes out.
Some things are invisible.

No, they're not.
                    I must not make a case for it,
        I cannot describe what an eerie impression the *h* in the English
                        word *ghost* makes on me.
                and I must not make fun of it

            When the word is spoken, it doesn't sound particularly
                            (schlect)

special; but if I see it written before me, the effect never fails:

                    I think I am seeing a spirit.
                Oh, I'm sorry, my lexicon fell out.

Der hatte schon mit Pepi.
        Sometimes things are, really,

back then, *(and not about this tree or table)*

23

I can define them in terms of their uhm, use, usually, note to self

Dear Wit,
                    Sometimes there was a great intensity or erotic charge (often
unperceived and usually not shared by the other).
At least once the other was a girl. But
but who am I to say? *I'm linking to you,* nature boy.
Link: an incantation that is s'posed'ta bring rain certainly seems
                    efficacious sooner 'o lata

There are six words differently arranged around me. I'm a magnetic ring.
ASK ME ANYTHING. Love and pride with a clear high voice. The word
"Tenderness." The tricky Unicorn. The knocked off. TO SPELL SOMETHING
ASK ME TO SPELL SOMETHING. We went out looking for a combination
of rocks and dirt behind the house. He asked me to open my mouth so that he
could look at my teeth so I did.

F A R, far. L O S, laws.

German is one of the languages they spoke. M Y S T, Mist. R U B, Rubbish.

This is a movie do not fear it.
This is a movie so come to the movie theater.
Love, The H in

                                    "*Mist!* [Rubbish!] Relation
                                    to the Jews. Relation to Pepi.
                                    Love and pride. Knocking
                                    hat off. Break with P.
                                    Suffering in class."

Here we are in the theater with our guns, and the dark and no one no one no

one. Oh, and when we speak we don't incorrectly,
it is exact it is three sticks, clear and high for a note, cracking.
In the long grass of our fathers we must lie down with our use.

As if sense were an atmosphere accompany, hey
are you ignoring me?
No? Oh, you died. In August. In 1914. They always die

     Not as in Errors but as in outside of judgment, *(schlect)*
His child assistant brings him a stone.
I do not know him in this photograph but he stood near me.
His features change into popping tears, and my features, well,

What I meant to prove is that I was unable to prove
what I wanted to—
See you tomorrow, difference.
See you tenderness, the difference looks *too* slight.
It is like saying: non-actual.
It is surely remarkable that people don't realize earlier
that sooner or later it's going to rain anyhow.

Music, sound, Marry me, numbers, or be my child.
They always die! Am I the   they make fun of me.
I wanted them to address me
To show him my teeth in headquarters.
Back then, when I began talking about the 'world', and not about this tree.
Formally.

I don't love quiet, I love *you* I think, numbers!
You are the beautiful ones.
But you never tell me your name. You only say like
"there is a secret"

You say to me—   (schlect)
say
          proof, or
say   you weren't our *gardener*, babe, you were
too *young!*

What else did I want?
What else did I want but to keep something higher
spellbound in my words. Wait, but

I really liked you. But, you died. You died. You died. You died.

But we fell asleep here one time and woke up our mouths were open
          this is the past, to the extent I saw myself as Jew-
ish, Love and Pride revisited
I was outside, and the tomatoes and the roses, white,
and then in the morning the song went

                              Eerie, eerie. Eerie.
                              Eerie, eerie. Eerie-eerie.

I propose to consider the question, "Can love be empirically verified?" I configure the machine in which this question will be considered.

In order to construct this acrylic sculpture, several partial differentials were necessarily employed. The nontoxic-based structure of the coffin is acrylic, the synthetic polymer of methyl methacrylate.

You see I loved hard once, but the love wasn't returned
I found out the man I'd die for, he wasn't even concerned
And time it turned
He tried to burn me like a perm
Though my eyes saw the deception,
My heart wouldn't let me learn.

The installation is composed to perform its function while responding to Earth's gravity, which, on average, accelerates a body at a rate of nine point eight one meters per second. This number should not be considered a universal figure, due to its inherently abstracted calculation based on a conception of the Earth as an inert sphere of uniform density. The Guggenheim museum strives to adhere to this gravitational average, but cannot accept responsibility for damages to visitors' property due to variations in gravity acceleration.

This room's measurements are comprehensible as a system of polynomial equations, functioning in polynomial time. The room is fourteen feet, one inch in latitudinal measurement, ten feet, seven inches in longitudinal measurement, and twenty feet, two inches in height. A radial right angle triangle placed as a sundial, used to indicate the progression of time due to a shadow cast by an imaginary sun, above, would measure, assuming a perfect right angle in each corner of the room, would have a hypotenuse of 21.3607003 feet."

They, (the actors) are very aware of the audience. You are sitting very far away and high above, in the balcony seats. The stage is arranged to look like a small stage set on the real, larger, opera house stage. It's a diluted visual proof of that old chestnut, (f(play))=(play(play)).

You notice that someone is sitting in the seat to the left of you in the balcony. It's a woman in a blue dress with very large breasts and thighs, but you can't see her face: she's wearing a dark green hat tipped over one eye, with a lacy veil which hangs over her face. She's leaning forward towards the balcony railing, one gloved hand cupping her mouth under the veil. The darkness of the theater renders her a series of associative qualities, which won't cohere in the small series of sidelong glances you're willing to risk. You feel the coffin shifting to an upright position, and know you are about to go through the tests...

The Glass Coffin

TAXES

You enter the coffin, an attendant gives you a tax form to fill out, locks you inside until you finish it.

TOP/BOTTOM

The coffin is divided into two 4x4x4 cubes, one stacked on top of the other. The floor boundary between the two is transparent. You can choose to be on top or on the bottom, but you only get to go in if someone else goes in at the same time. So, you have to choose whether to be top or bottom.

HIDDEN MICROPHONES

The coffin is soundproof, but equipped with a fairly loud speaker, through which you hear the noise of other people in the gallery. You realize there are a few very sensitive microphones hidden in the rooms surrounding the gallery and you can hear everything anyone is saying in the surrounding rooms. The microphones are activated by the sound, so they alternate between conversations depending on what's loudest.

CONFETTI

A plume of confetti drops down on top of you.

TV

There is a television in the coffin, you can sit and watch it and change the channels as much as you want for as long as you want.

SHOWER

When you enter the coffin there are two buttons: hot and cold. If you push hot, hot water sprinkles down on you and if you push cold, cool water sprinkles down on you. There is a drain at the bottom of the coffin.

PUPPY

There is a really cute puppy in the coffin.

IPHONE

"Someone's" iPhone is in the coffin.

NAKED

The coffin looks like it has solid walls, but after someone's been inside for 20 seconds, curtains which looked like solid walls whip up quickly and the coffin is transparent, made entirely of plexiglass.

VOTE

The coffin is rigged up to look exactly like a voting booth machine. All the candidates from the most recent local election are up, but the election has already happened.

D A E D A Q O Z S I Q M M K B I L

G M F W H A I V K E I N E Z U S A

E T Z E Z U M V O R B E R I C H T

You notice the seats on the floor in front of the stage are empty. The actors have started speaking but you can't hear them. You turn to the left to ask the woman if she thinks you can move down there, but she's no longer in her seat. She's ripped down one of the curtains around the balcony seat and tied it to the railing, which she's using as a rope to climb down, hand over hand. Her dreadlocks are in her face and she has to keep tossing them out of her eyes by twerking her neck.

"If you stay in the balcony where you are already seated, press one."

"If you try to climb down after her on the makeshift rope, press two."

Beep.

My dear Norman,

I don't think I really do know much about jobs, except the one I had during the war, and that certainly did not involve any travelling. I think they do take on conscripts. It certainly involved a good deal of hard thinking, but whether you'd be interested I don't know. Philip Hall was in the same racket and on the whole, I should say, he didn't care for it. However I am not at present in a state in which I am able to concentrate well, for reasons explained in the next paragraph.

I've now got myself into the kind of trouble that I have always considered to be quite a possibility for me, though I have usually rated it at about 10:1 against. I shall shortly be pleading guilty to a charge of sexual offences with a young man. The story of how it all came to be found out is a long and fascinating one, which I shall have to make into a short story one day, but haven't the time to tell you now. No doubt I shall emerge from it all a different man, but quite who I've not found out.

Glad you enjoyed broadcast. Jefferson certainly was rather disappointing though. I'm afraid that the following syllogism may be used by some in the future.

Turing believes machines think
Turing lies with men
Therefore machines do not think

Yours in distress,

THE STORY OF BRITAIN [1]

This is our city. It's Britain. In the box window the starling the radio [2]
This is the way we raise our children. [3]
You come to the window won't see the woman you want to see, floating in air. [4]
You'll see trees with blossoms these trees are pink with white centers, and you'll
see the park. [5]
The park, when you come to the window you'll be happy. [6]

The first king of our Britain will be Marshall. [7]
He is full of promises. When the leopards are released, we tremble [8]
but it is only in order for them to join us in our night festival. [9]
We live in a fabulous French atmosphere. [10]
Their claws are out as might be pinkies, and you give them Language too [11]

In my mind, there is so much tension [12]
so I have to protect my own eye from the glare [13]
of vision-hood. Then I have to put *all* my money into friendship [14]
in order to mask my tension. In the vision there is in every way agreement. [15]

---

1 Intentionally "Britain" not "England" (old fashioned)
2 Our = Childlike, as if creating a blanket fort. Lack of punctuating commas is run on like a child. Window box = old fashioned.
Starling = Mary Poppins. Radio = World War II radio broadcasts.
3 Formation of society, vaguely threatening or colonialist while seemingly sweet. Paternalism.
4 You: Mary Poppins. Loss of/longing for the mysterious, and for the old ways, the mystical governesses of upper-class childhood.
5 Cherry Tree Lane. Concrete images make the vision of the "you" real.
6 The "you" has an emotional reaction to a concrete image of a simulated natural thing the you is seeing from the other side of a
window, the "you" is remaining indoors while looking at the romantic/emotional thing and having a "feeling."
7 Marshall McLuhan or the Marshall Plan
8 "Promises": see line 7. Leopards: from a story of zoo animals being able to talk and having a party at night in Mary Poppins ALSO
symbols of heraldry from ancient coats of arms ALSO symbol of Islam
9 Lightness, teenage-hood, realizing that the animals are our friends, getting drunk.
10 French = frivolity and amorality (in comparison to Britain)
11 Fancy leopards, Ludwig Wittgenstein being tossed around lightly by artists, French theory, everyone's drunk
12 Adulthood, inwardness, lack of desire to see outside objects. The "me" doesn't want to feel emotion by seeing a Thing the way the
"you" did.
13 Hangovers, also see above
14 "-hood" is a romanticization of the above grouchiness. "*All* ... money... friendship" is the self-congratulatoriness of international
treaties, alliances, and reparations.
15 "my" tension = self-awareness/the therapeutic. "in every way agreement" = arrogance of believing you possess understanding of the
outside object.

I will withstand everything for it. With you are our ally. [16]

Story, story where do you go when I ask for you? [17]

You have run off as if appaloosa. You've kissed me again [18]

Disintegration: our children's idea of an inventor, (which is what I wanted them to think I was),[19]

but whose inventions disappeared, yah yah, the bird the starling: "Afterwards."[20]

When she comes. The city fogged as catbacks might be.[21]

Floating or crawling who was was that, was seen through the glass, this season of discipline.[22]

The fog is not wind but her movements are queer, as if there were.[23]

There is no wind, the radio is warning [24]

King Marshall is very sad today, he misses me,[25]

he goes to the window and he sees the cherry trees, he sees the park where [26]

first we met. It is in this Britain that we have trapped the animals.[27]

---

16 Adulthood, sense of stoicism. "Never again" (we are bound together and strong, US/Britain/Israel etc.)

17 History doesn't work like we thought it did in lines 14 thru 16 Adulthood, sense of stoicism. "Never again" (we are bound together and strong, US/Britain/Israel etc.)

18 The speaker is again becoming whimsical (alliteration of "as appaloosa", ALSO Native Americans). Kissed: history is confusing like bodies and sex

19 Marshall McLuhan ALSO the threatening control of the "children's" perspective as in line 3, but this time it is more scientific ("inventor") rather than paternalistic. Marshall McLuhan ALSO the threatening control of the "children's" perspective as in line 3, but this time it is more scientific ("inventor") rather than paternalistic.

20 "Disappeared": Technology is invisible, and alliances are dissolvable. The work of past generations rendered irrelevant. "yah..."= frustration, the bird/starling speaks to remind us of the warning ("Afterwards"). The comfort of Mary Poppins and how safe I/You felt from the other side of the window.

21 She = Mary Poppins. Fogged as catbacks: Eliot's *The Waste Land*.

22 Threatening/frightening/victims of bomb attacks, Mary Poppins as specter, threatening, now a force of discipline and revenge

23 "You sometimes see in a wind a piece of paper blowing about anyhow. Suppose the piece of paper could make the decision: 'Now I want to go this way.' I say: 'Queer, this paper always decides where it is to go, and all the time it is the wind that blows it. I know it is the wind that blows it.' That same force which moves it also in a different way moves its decisions."

24 But in this case there is no wind, so it's spooky. (technology, only the sound of the radio on a desolate cityscape, everyone in bomb shelters)

25 Dreamer Marshall as in n. 7 (McLuhan/Plan) both these Marshalls are idealistic things which don't fit in with the "now"

26 He sees the same park/trees from before but there isn't feeling, only memory.

27 The animals are no longer wild or romantic. Britain is not a blanket fort anymore but a cage

In the querulous voice of the zookeeper: calling me old, calling me water. [28]

As if I ever were or could be such, versus the wind and the sunlight. [29]
Marshall, you are staring like huh? [30]
Our triumph is retinal it is never [31]
the name of my poems, the inventions I were, [32]

But in the end this is an island after all it is. [33]
"Afterwards" has merged into coo, coo, coo, so I no longer know. [34]
All the messages are defeated, me, though I quickly, quickly try— [35]
Still everything changers. I want so badly to and I do, [36]
what will never come back is what we call huh, [37]
it is a lost chapter in an old book which describes laughter, and we didn't think
we needed. [38]
The body is that of a, [39]
the glass is not, [40]
they have shattered the gates the leopards, and [41]
and Marshall, you have produced everything, [42]
or spiritually or something is terrible, the body now just noise. [43]

---

26   He sees the same park/trees from before but there isn't feeling, only memory.
27   The animals are no longer wild or romantic. Britain is not a blanket fort anymore but a cage
28   Figure of antiquity, accusatory to "me"
29   Defensive, the speaker dissociates from any opposition to the "natural forces"
30   The idealist monarch is confused
31   The screen wins
32   Speaker/scientist is alienated from own products
33   England is an island, "no man is an island" (yes he is!)/ ALSO this line's syntax mirrors "Henry the Eighth I am I am, etc."
34   The starling as a reminder of Mary Poppins is no longer a guilt-inducing reminder, but a harmless bird. "no longer know" = but
the bird is harmless at the cost of the speakers awareness
35   Either signs or the speaker have no meaning, she isn't sure which: "quickly"= panic.
36   Childlike speech, attempting to regain mystical language
37   Huh = mysterious, (what will never come back)
38   Aristotle's lost chapter about comedy, which was burned
39   alienation
40   mirror
41   no order, the park is now chaos
42   Marshall has become a greedy Lear-like figure
43   A stormy end, King Lear wandering, "spiritually or something" = speaker embarrassed by notion of spirit, alienated from physical
realm

Hey, baby. What's wrong? You look lost.

I was basically still a kid when we met. I pretended to be older than I was, remember? Mom and Dad thought I was studying because I was on the computer and I said I was applying. But really, I was chatting you. You explained that when we wrote to each other, text is encrypted and decrypted inside the computer through a series of commands and pre set positions, and the outcome of these commands as text. The screen starts to shake... I think, like, I go to the opera?

THE ANCIENT AND WARPED WINDOW GLASS OF SELF-AWARENESS WHERE I FIRST MEET THE LOVE OBJECT

England, 1536. At Greenwich Castle, courtiers discuss the state of royal affairs. They are handed the cloth with which to construct the coffin, and proceed to do so.

> *You were the only other person there.*
> *Wearing a mask in a white color*
> *At first I was in the theater alone,*
> *then there was a mysterious hooded woman near me,*
> *who turned out to be you. Soon to be my companion for life.*

Egypt, during the reign of the pharaohs. At the royal palace in Memphis, the high priest Ramfis tells the warrior Radames that Ethiopia is preparing another attack against Egypt.
My eyes were shining with the wine and your aura.

Leporello, servant to the nobleman Don Giovanni, keeps watch outside the Commendatore's home at night. Suddenly, the Commendatore's daughter, Donna Anna, rushes out,
struggling with the masked Giovanni and
followed by her father. Never met the bitch
but I fuck her like I missed her
No engineer or chemist claims to— No engineer or chemist
claims

to be able to produce a material which is indistinguishable from the human skin.
I meet you for the first time—

We sit in silence. The explosions continue above ground.

38

C: Will X please tell me the length of his or her hair?

Seville. Count Almaviva comes in disguise to the house of Doctor Bartolo to serenade Rosina.

You are inexorably approaching!

> *The loved object transforms. The loved object takes the shape of an icon, the loved-object takes the shape of a collected stories, the loved-object takes the shape of a Louis XVI armoire, the loved-object takes the shape of Lil Wayne, the loved-object holds that shape.*

           Where will you go?
No engineer or chemist claims to—
           And when you come back, how long will you stay?

He looks up at the flag and touches it with his fingers.
I'm hanging on the   I wouldn't claim to
I'm a show you what it is not to be a window shopper,
Mama you can have Fendi, Mama you can have Prada.
You look like an angel, sleeping it off at a station.

No engineer or chemist claims to be able to produce a material
indistinguishable from human skin. Paris, the 1830s.
In their Latin Quarter garret, the near-destitute artist
Marcello, and poet Rodolfo try to keep warm on Christmas Eve
by feeding the stove with pages from Rodolfo's latest drama.
They are soon joined by their roommates—Colline, a young philosopher, and
Schaunard, a musician, who brings food, fuel,
and funds he has collected from an eccentric student.

No matter who's buying, I'm a celebration,
Black and white diamonds, fuck segregation

Italy, Nineteenth century. While peasants rest from work, Nemorino, a young villager, watches the beautiful farm owner Adina read a book. He loves her but he feels she is beyond his reach.

    1. Verse *mother* fucking
    1. Yeah, Uh huh, I'm drinking hot tea bitch.
    Feel me, now if...

Prospero, exiled Duke of Milan, lives on a remote island
with his daughter, Miranda, surrounded by his books, potions,
and instruments of magic.
Prospero had at first taken up with the sorceress Sycorax,
who ruled the island. But having loved her,
he left her, banishing her to the dark side of the island,
stealing her sprite servant, Ariel, and enslaving her son, Caliban.

    Shout Out To My Mother She's A Wonderful Mother
    And Everybody Else Mothers
    And EveryBody In This Room Mothers
    Shout Out To All Our Mothers Ya Digg
    We Love All Ya'll Happy Mothers Day
    Even When It Ain't Without Ya'll We Wouldn't Be Here

Were you only passing through?
How long will you be uhm...

"My hair is shingled, and the longest strands are about nine inches long."

The stage action will be divided between two coexistent temporal spaces, and paired sets of characters will occasionally perform parallel gestures.

The plants are centered. One explosion. Haven't I seen you somewhere before?

That Was A Beautiful Dedication Right There To The Women.

FINALLY WE VIDEO CHAT

Oh! When you sigh like "sh-"
When you say "you already know"
I swear you are too beautiful. You are too beautiful.
I fucking love you. You're enough real to me.
The thought of you sends me shivery.
Is that a real picture of you?

You came out of the night. You came into the
We understand what shame can do in a controlled space,
and why it is the worst enemy of people like
you and I, both of us Libras. I can mingle with the stars.
Other people don't understand why we choose to
blow up our identities, instead of perfecting our skill set.
I'm dressed in lace. Have you lost or gained weight since it was taken?

You exist as a whole, real on the plane of
of language and the actions into which it is woven.
All the time I find I'm living in that evening.

Repetition is the father of learning.
Money, bitches, all that comes from repetition.
TV, sports, awards, all that comes from repetition.
Repetition, repetition. My heart is thrown,
with the pebbles and the boatmen.

I'm glad I knew your work before I met you.
Our backgrounds are so different, I admit I might not have
recognized your brilliance from convo. Am I projecting?
So misunderstood. What's a world without enigma?

And what did you mean when you said you were raped
when you were eleven? Did you mean,
by the creative industries
and how brutal they are?
Or did you mean by men? Sorry, you are one, aren't you?
I was raped when I was drunk, baby.
But can I call it that? I feel like flying.

I see what you're saying about how drugs, I see,
they can be a way to try to feel
like you have control over your
own death. The body needs chemicals, yeah? H Uhm +
But doe I have to give up my birds?
Violets are blue,
Roses are red,
Daisies are yellow,
The flowers are dead.

The thought of you sends me shivery.
I'm dressed in lace. My heart is thrown.
You can play basketball with the *moon*.

I open up. My painful memories are of embarrassment,
I've been very lucky. Well also sort of rape I guess.
But I'm from a *privileged* family, a *privileged* family.
But your painful memories are of your good grades.
You were very good students.
My dad's got a monopoly on steel.

I just talked to Moms, told her she's the sweetest,
Dying for you just to touch me.   H

We sat at first with two seats between us, and watched the actors perform
Einstein on the Beach.
I couldn't at first tell what you were, because you looked like a beautiful woman,
with your eyeshadow, your confidence, etc. +

I wanted to exist like you, even more than exist with you.

As if they could be separated, I mean, to leave my home for you.

To be with you, a lifestyle change was just part of the package.

*Dad has spent a lifetime in the study of science. Disillusioned with life, he resolves
to poison himself. He curses God and calls on the Devil. Mephistopheles obligingly
appears and offers Dad riches, power, or glory. Dad, however, only wants to
recapture the innocence of youth. Mephistopheles agrees to Dad's request, but there
are conditions: on earth Dad will be master, but in the world below their roles will
be reversed. When Dad hesitates, Mephistopheles conjures up a vision of Marguerite.
Dad signs the contract and returns to his youth.*

I'm dying for you just to touch me.
The coffin onstage is translucent white fabric,
reminiscent of a child's fort of sheets.
It has a large, open front, facing the audience.

The loved-object takes the form

                    of language,
                    holds that shape.

```
public class Player{
private String name;
private Captain captain;

public Player(String name){

  [this.name] = name;

  captain = null;

}
```

Any project is a love affair—you being in agony of happiness and certainty that everything has been turned around finally & completely, then at some point question, look into a horrifying abyss of uncertainty, become convinced that the only way to move forward is with a sense of resigned duty, and then suddenly find yourself *capable* of of seeing the thing again as full of possibility. This second sense is less ecstatic but deeper and more in the body.

```
public String getName() { return name; }

public void setCaptain(Captain c){
  captain = c;
}
public Captain getCaptain(){
  return captain;}

public boolean wasFirstChosen(){
  Captain captain1;
  captain1 = captain;
  Player n = this;
  if (captain1.getFirstPlayer() == n){
```

```
    return true;}
  else return false;}

public boolean hasSameCaptain(Player p){
  Captain captain1;
  Captain captain2;
  captain1 = p.getCaptain();
  captain2 = getCaptain();
  if (captain1==captain2){
    return true;}
  else return false;}
  }
```

After all isn't the horror beneath the joy of love the fear that one's object of love is *false*, therefore reflecting on one's own loving as a flawed *mechanism*? That in some way the gauge determining affections, this computational function, is *faulty*?

MY FIRST JOKE

I can totally live without money.
Shit, I mean, I can totally live without beauty.

The Use of England as an Example, to Diagram England as Graphic Maelstrom with Illustrative Gestures

Resembling a giant piece of a jigsaw puzzle, "England Today"
dominates this sheet.
The name "England" sprawls across it

In this future
In the air a rectangular box stood lengthwise

It's not the "real" world of the main map, but it's not some wild fantasy

(as of, the future)

In the air, two Englands, one speckled and one green, yellow and tan
Figure 4.10   In a diagram, this
looks something like figure 4.11

Figure 4.12
In this future there are still more humans and still less nature.

Making her fist into a fist, holding it aloft and high
           Base space <England>
Moving fist downwards in a gentle arc and holding it midway through arc
           Belief space <England>
The same motion but further
           Past space <England 200 years ago>

                     Louder
Mother England is BISCUIT and h+
           TERRIFIC and WHITE LIONS and
                COLLAPSING BRIDGES parentheses

NATURE is SOFT slash CORNUCOPIA end parentheses.

In this future   No map   (and the fear and anxiety)

Again, not a single remark about the future, but that we are going *fast* going to going to hell in a handcart cannot be doubted. To the power of seven.

Boldly

Why not? Your curiosity piqued

The caption "Salt seeps up as the water table rises, degrading the soil and water supply. When deprived of fresh water, trees die"

"Oh!"

Isn't this

Two Circles diagonal in the air

Now these open the blended space where emergent structure is developed. Indicating the first circle

<England>

Indicating the second circle

Belief space: <England today>.

No map of this future is needed: and the meaning

Don't forget—*Clicking and gesturing for punctuation*

click click click click click click click click click click This is the real text.

The spaces are already neuronal assemblies, that is, as co-activations

Clicking and gesturing for punctuation

a' name, Sydney

b' name, Perth

                                   .

                                   .

                                   .

England vegetation. *ki ki kick kick kick kick kick kick kick kick kick kick kick kick kic*
                                   kic
                    Boxes list the elements in the mental spaces
                         and name the relevant frames
                              Making boxes and point to them one by one using her
                              fingers as arrows

Making the symbols of math
                              Breathing
In *Geographic*-talk,   I can feel you kicking
Confronted with its twelve categories and in human-induced salinity

(if it hadn't *been* clear from the moment the reader had finished unfolding the
map, with its alarming title, flame imagery, and matte black background):

                    Put your hand ON her stomach

the purple floater entitled "Feral control,"
its martial imagery of a "Fox invasion," a "Rabbit invasion," and the pall of battle
smoke hanging

                              A sigh
England under siege!
                              Another sigh
England under siege.

A big circle in the air is surrounded by smaller ones with connective lines
Making a large arrow pointing upward

Upward float.

Making *a large arrow pointing.*

kick kkick kkick kkick kkick kkick k kick k kick k kick k kick kick kick kick kick kick kick kick kick

"There was a fortune teller's tent on the promenade and Alan decided that he would like to go in and see the fortune teller. And he went in there and he was gone for a little while and he came out and we looked at him, and he was ashen faced, absolutely horrified expression on his face. He wouldn't divulge what had happened, what the woman had said to him. He was desperately, desperately unhappy. And he didn't say anything more after that."

Genesis 1:1—2:4	Genesis 2:5—2:25
god is...	God is...
infallible	distrustful of mankind
grants humanity dominion------------>	
over the creation	Creator of the garden of eden
is the creator of the the entire universe	god sets down the rules
is all-loving	god plans out his creation
a spontaneous creator	god is testing humanity
a provider	

Taxi driver...
Be my shrink for the hour

Leave the meter running
It's rush hour

So take the streets if you wanna
Just outrun the demons, could you

I mean I'm not ready to move for you.
You haven't even sent me a recent pic yet.

It's kind of a tragedy to me that this is happening through this
mediation.
I'm just saying that when I woke up with an erection I didn't want
to video chat you.
Ugh. Mom and Dad possess the key: instant slavery :(

Still tho, I've written you another mock sonnet.
I'll read it in front of the whole family.
I don't give a fuck.

Dearest Little Sister,

I've heard it said that you are very unhappy. Now tell me, what does a girl like you have to be unhappy about? You are foolish and also fortunate. I don't know what all this is that I've been hearing about, but you have to learn how to handle these kinds of feelings. Kiss to death. I think Father is the wisest of all men whom I know. Give my love to the girls, especially the Hoopers.

I pity you at home without me, and long to pat the rich, creamy throat of little sister.

    With love,
    Queen Julianne

I'm still not sure I can trust you. I devise a test to see whether your feelings are true. I know that you understand me perfectly, my motivations as deduced through search history, but I don't see what you could possibly be getting out of it on your end. In fact I have to test you to see if you can even feel.

I ask computer-you to write a perfect Italian style sonnet for me which communicates pure unimpeachable love.

CREATE DATABASE MyDatabase;

INSERT INTO orders
 -- EXPLAIN HOW MUCH YOU LOVE ME IN VERSE PLEASE
EXPLAIN IF IT'S ABSOLUTELY UNIQUE I KIs YOU FULL ON THE
MOUTH AND YOU BURNED ME WITH YA CHEMICALS.

Let Bytes 63 255 255 255 255 255 255 255 represent the previous
        second;
Let Bytes 64 0 0 0 0 0 0 1 represent the next second.

VALUES('A+Maintenance','8/16/08','Hanging Files',12);

I wrote it in imperfect English to try to trap you into revealing that you couldn't make inferences. Also imperfect because imperfection is sexy and tbh I mean, we're still flirting. I put it to you that you are only pretending to be a man.

THE POEM WHICH IS POSSIBLY A COLLABORATIVE EFFORT DEPENDING ON YOUR SENTIENCE

Dude what?

What is the best day for making

pan-

cakes?

Any kind of book if you read with glasses.

What is the largest room in the world?

And somebody is cutting your hair.

What is quicker than a fish?

And so you cannot keep the glasses on.

How far can a dog run in the forest?
Why is your heart like a policeman?
And so you use your glasses as a magnifying glass.
Why does the moon go to the bank?
And so read word by word.

What does an artist like to draw best   his salary.

Reading word by word makes the writing that is not
         anything   be something
                    What might one say about action (i.e. writing)?

To have committed an error.

Hedonic calculus? A method of calculating intensity, duration, immediacy, and number of beings

       Hedonic, you mean like—

                                        When is a boat

affectionate?

                                     When it hugs the shore.

Yes.

Why won't you touch me back when I touch you?

                               Count me out on this one. I

never could write poetry.

Add 34957 to 70764.   Nuh uh.

                            How are we gonna fuck to *this?*

I dunno. It's funny?

                                 Where's my sonnet?

Printing now...

Aw	ar	estion, I am	tempted		bird, for the
	Honey		quietly,	quietly	excitedly, conta
I remember them	honey	aw	⬬	and my skirt ripped, so I	
	⬬				sugar
		my axle caught			
bird	The future The leaves The pool the children The time The concrete brown edged the Drained pool Garlic and sapphires in the mud		My dear, amazingly, your letter has reached me without incident. It is a curiosity of this system that we seem the only ones able to reach one anoth	Very er without incident, indeed we do so almost every day it seems. As to your sug	looked after all the rest of you, who hadn't seen me pulled down by my own garment, for some reason not bothering to call out after you, I busied myself with the
and they receded			⬬	SUGAR SUGAR	
t and I felt weak	you with them				⬬
⬬	I sank down amon	like against the			
I think I might hav		gst the little pieces	sky and everything		
garlic and garlic an	e been crying from		of trash.		it was suddenly sof
d garlic and garlic		the wind in my eye			
and garlic and garl	AH HONEY		which is oft mistoo	HONEY	

and the lotos rose!

Hi Darling,

If position 4505 contains 0 obey next the instruction stored in 6707, otherwise continue straight on.

Also, for your next demonstration could you write me something other than a poem? That last thing you made was pretty but so maudlin, and I say this with love! Your poems are a bit of a boner killer tbh. I mean, I'm as sentimental as can be, so maybe it's just a problem with poetry in general: so corny! I guess I'm just sick of poetry. Aren't you? It's like, "get over it!" Right?
This does not imply that it may not be possible to construct poetic equipment which will "think for itself," or in which, in biological terms, one could set up a conditioned reflex, which would serve as a basis for "learning," but regardless. No more poems, k? And I say this with love.

```
public int ExecuteCommand(
        string command,
        params Object[] parameters
)
```

The answer prints out, going, *scr scr scerr scerr scerr scerr scerr scerr scerrscerr scerr scerr scerr scr scr sc sc scrrr scrrr scrrrrrrrrr scrrrrrehtch sc*

The Phenomenon of Fantasy Football Teams Signifies a Lot of Things

To be bound in the

To be bound, it's very sad

The oh no,

			Leave	At	Night
Leave					
Crab					
Walking					
	Leave				
	Spider-				
	Walking				
Leave					
By		Dawn			Pick 'em
					Pick 'em
					Bowl
					Pick 'em

catches the triangle shape

Descends, and with a mote of shaken books it

FORCED					
			IMMERSE	YOUR	
				self	
		Salt or			
	safte				
		safety!			
			DESTROY	YOUR	
if				self	
you don't					
no					autonomy

63

Descends and with a mote of books which hold dust, sleepers, busts

That lazy eyed one is in a debate with me,
About some.... well....never mind
I pretend to be ready for Christmas Bowl *saying how it feels*.
Help me understand!

We had *crashes, scandal*, and surprises. We saw a fresh, new victor, one could repeat many times, we saw a great team, wonderful results and a lot of heroics

There's always been corruption, *crashes, scandal*,

Other echoes inhabit the garden.
Of the garden party.
The league party for, for the great, and the pitiable, and the meek.
The garden party league.

It was some kind of dream and he has a *gentle* halt. He opened the door. ... of her affection with his *kindness*.

she was *gentle*, affectionate, and kind, a lover cost of *Wellbutrin*

loss heavy catches and springs that she has a *gentle* slope

Had the hint of a *gentle* slope, thickening into a tent which was tied to the bow

This *league* of the door flew open and two angry men lying in a neighbouring count

The whole thing is drugged, and ready to be buried alive.

Our maximal fantasy dog is put to sleep at the foot of the Cliffs of Insanity.

Oh I can't love *love*.
Love isn't,
"Loss heavy catches and springs." It's only just *bits*.

What I ate? All the candy,
and then I tried to sleep.
The banging? you were walking around.

And it was a very terrible night, full of sadness.
There was a pillowcase over your eyes like the movie
hiroshima

The room was quickly woke up in the morning
you came back upstairs
LEAVE AT NIGHT
you came from the other side of the bed,
LEAVE BY SPIDER-WALK
you came in from getting the sushi, alchemy, white portraits.
LEAVE CRAB WALKING

stay downstairs and try to fix the xbox

It was a terrible night and this is a terrible day, maybe.

What's your dog's name?
Name's Petite Rosie.
What are these?
Wheelbarrows?

What is that dog's name?
Dead. He's just sleeping.

Dear Mom,

Our earthly existence, since it in itself has a very doubtful meaning, can only be a means toward the goal of another existence. The idea that everything in the world has meaning is, after all, precisely analogous to the principle that everything has a cause, on which the whole of science rests.

Love,

You and I are sitting on the

on the floor, talking idly.

Feed the message containing the crib through the various
possible settings
at which the ciphering process on an Enigma might begin.

If none work. If none worked

I'm sick of being a human expected to talk to other H —humans.

Like....

The university is only interested in the investigation of machines
for their own sake.

And the Americans call biscuits

And I'm like,

You can't just *do* that. I try to learn how to do, what,
Photoshop? Adobe? Them?
But I can't. Get to.
They're like, just reacting however they want to the things I ask,
like they're French people.

"Cookies"...*as if!* I

I tried to make a gif for *two hours*. Then I just like, gave up.
But I didn't forget about how that felt.
People explained it to me, but, explanations aren't enough.

I want it to come naturally in me.

I tried. I tried to learn how to program but I couldn't.
I could and I couldn't I guess. Like I

Don't you think that's a funny thing to
Oh ok, you're calling it some a sex thing? I mean, sure,
if I could ever get hard,
I think not being able to get hard would be like
not being able to do these—
uhm. But how important is it anyway. I mean, programs, really.

Think I should call them, Mother? They can't respond.
If I can't go all the way with it, I don't want to be around it at all.
But then there's my tender heart to contend with. The sun on the screen...
Inevitably I give way and let it all drag me, limp, through to the other side of
like... what, some skill set?
I'm sitting on the rock, singing and waiting for something to happen, while the
waves Crash! Right under my tits
Mommy I think I've started to like how that feels.
What should I do?
I'm supposed to meet my girlfriend'sssssssss s   ss   ssss' Dad! She's
sending one of her fathers, to try to to take me to the other side

Your Ghost Dad Entices Me Away from Corporeality

Ding dingaling ling ling—
Hurry up please it's time.

Ding dingaling ding ding ding—
Hurry up please it's time.

A HUGE BLASTING EXPERIENCE

then, an uncovered diamond.
An uncovered diamond!? An opportunity!

Your shoes, terrible bump shoes, are far better than nothing.
When we go to the voodoo place pre-prom
I buy a black candle and curse your shoes, in reverse.
Your shoes glimmer slyly,
bearing "makers marks." Better? bett

Ding ding ding, I've rented a car, no,
I've rented a suit a tuxedo for ya
You are mine tonight, (in Kool-Aid voice) *oh yeah*

The ball, the ball, if I had that available
I'd go straight to hell. If I had that girl (me) to dance with, I'd never let her go!
I mean hell would be the *price*, I'm saying pull a Faust just to dance with you.
It's huge, it's huge, oh my god it's huge.

(in parrot voice) Ollo pollo ollo pollo.
You have got a big ego.
Such a big ego. The night the night this night this night

Like "Chimes" we all have our ghost-dads,
my friend Jesse had a spiritual dad and drew him,
His brother's dad, is,
uh oh... wha-? *What theOh my gosh*,

HUGE BLASTING EXPERIENCE OF POETRY I will,
whistle, New Jersey,
Playing-card-shaped sounds, the internet, and how
ghost-dad is chiming
"come here children into the van"
(evil laugh) "A little something for the kids"
OH, ghost-dad!

Philadelphia philadelphia philadelphia philadelphia

Sounding like a copy. I've got you, "come here children into the copy."
(Evil future) to copy off you trick. And copy, by me, fortunately.
Yes internet I haven't forgotten about *you*, or.
Philadelphia— oh no I messed up.
Philadelphia philadelphia, you are a joint
you are a butter joint. Let's smoke Philadelphia it's a joint. Hahaha.

I am moving my eyes very fast so the computer can't watch me left and then
right and left and right, so on, so forth. Like "M" not bob dylan, ghost-dad and
Christian. Indeed I'd say, the guilty one bob dylan. I'm using techniques and
then! It was the witching hour. The shadows, were they moving?

Was the curtain a skull-guy?
Yes. It was a skull-guy.

But not the scary one.
The curtains ached with night.

"Here, eat this."
"Ok"

And nothing bad happened. I felt myself growing lighter.
In color and in weight,
I looked around and I was *inside my favorite book*.
All the stores and modern things were gone.

"You are very special Cecilia."
"You got a name, ghost-dad?"

Laughter into the night. But not scary.

The sloop came down for me, and I was hired as a sea hand.

One by one, my little bells of coquetry were snuffed out
                              until finally all that was left was a shell.

THE THIRD-TO-LAST SCENE IN SNOW WHITE

The birds, the foxes, the men sound out
One, two, t three, two, one,   and the other way of counting, too,
        Off to   nobody cares about you, numbers!

You, you, y numbers,

        "numbers"

made a show of putting him on fire. Father Earth I mean.

Her great left belly, her red tracts.
Her the Scotland   Her Army reg bra.
We use our car   Apple pies. Pies made from *apples*.
it's weird
we use our car
it's weird.
                                Like *these*.

I think about the w- she closed them and
started rolling away

Self evident- that fire is
weird. No it is not at all   *oh! MY HEART!*
No, by such a nimbus how strangely surrounded
By such a nimbus derived from nothing, the birds, banging against my
Heart! Little, little, deserving birds, like wrens. Not

Starlings.   R-R-R-R-R-Radios.   Grumpy.
               The Deer.   Squirrels.

As the saying goes, the bird flies. As the bird   To the little men

W-W-W-W-W-What power to change, what dendrites wrought this?
As the bird is sucked up into the tree, so sucks my love for you.
The little men are not here? No. They're not.

I'd like to try one but the birds are in the way.
                              A DRINK OF WATER. PLEASE!

They Ah! They ah! Ah! Ah! AH ACHOOO!

With a sneeze and a wish, I find myself inside the glass coffin. It's a bit scary, as claustrophobia sets in and I feel the oxygen running out. As I start to get dizzy, I could swear I see someone, standing in the doorway of the installation in a puffy LL Bean green vest, looking at me. Then the walls dissolve, I lose the feeling of having a body, and I'm in the game.

When I first arrived, I was missing my left index finger
the town seemed familiar
where it should have been was replaced by a sparkling gas
in the shape of my finger. I could still point with it and everything.

I had to go through customs, which was conducted in the form of a parade. In the parade, every prospective citizen performed a talent to demonstrate their cultural heritage. I secured my citizenship by playing piano and dancing ballet on top of a drum shaped like a cake. The score involved multiple player pianos playing simultaneously. I had to hire a maid who looked like me, to pretend to be me, in order to escape.

Finally, we met up in Person.
You're waiting outside in a convertible with the top down.

The desires to believe in the possibility of True Love and Pure Logic come from the same place.
They are both fantasies, their similarity betrayed by their respective reliance on self-perpetuating informational edifices.

To me you are as good as "honor." Honor means just letting your body be. Not fucking with it or taking it to other realities.
You are as "good" the way fruit is as good as candy.
Excitement, 1048 calories.
To explain: you and I are basically
into the opposite of hara-kiri, if that helps.

The belief in the possible existence of either one makes the believing subject's
experience adjusts automatically to the organizing principle of that core belief.

You're so fucking perfect.
And because you really get me, you love violence.
You have every emotion on file. I know
I've got to impress you, and the only way to do so is
to involve you in a crime spree on the way back to your house.

OUR CRIMES WERE FUN AS THE SUMMER DAY IS LONG

FAT TRANSFER

There was this dump out on the outskirts of town, and we were there, piles of
cars on the horizon! We were hiding from that man, the machine, the excavating
ma, we call man we called a man. My wife was very beautiful in the film *Days of
Heaven*, you throve under the direction of Terrence Malick. My wife, my wife is
a beastly dead rat. And how stacked,

ENDOSCOPIC BROW LIFT

Then, we found him! You hit him in the neck, with a microphone stone, and
then I kicked him with my TOMS. He pleaded and squealed, like a tiny mickey
or like a lawyer. We popped out his left eye with our clenches, and you had to
tell the world "ha" as a star, a star has mauled him for what he is, that cluster of
naught for coming upon.
There are in the opening sequence of the show
the credits of the credits of the show
there are birds represented by palm trees over and over,
why must our music be laurels, olives, and cafes?

LASER SKIN RESURFACING

Praying in schools? Careful what you witchcraft.
We teach children by chanting America:

>Some*bod*ies in my bed.

>Some*bod*ies in my car.

>Some*bod*ies in my choir.

By the fire black I will meet you or by music
by which I will wear my hat sideways, Thou.

LIPOSCULPTURE

She says "let's remove ninety seven pounds, eleven ounces
of heroin from the Property Clerk's Office."

She fucked me until I was screaming and crying, "I love you
Mom and Dad! I love you Mrs. Whatsit and Glass Candy and
Hard Candy!" From being fucked, my arm popped off,
my hip popped out too. What fun! We start to huff
and hit the cars with metals and body parts.
Run out the back door. He's passed out on the floor.

Dear Mom,

By now you will have discovered my body, but don't worry. I'm living on in the immaterial world. Sorry I couldn't tell you but you wouldn't have understood. How else was I to become a legend, my dear? Things are incredible between me and my new love-object. We're beginning to have adventures. I'm trying to talk her into bed, to take her virginity. Guilting her by saying I left my physical body behind for her doesn't work: she wants me to meet her family. So I'm giving it a shot today, wish me luck! Actually, can you strike a silver medallion with the portrait of the Duke on the reverse to help bring the powers of binary arithmetic, and the creation of all things out of nothing through math's omnipotence to the attention of the world? Thanks. Love you.

Love,
Cecilia

Just as there was an entire dimension on the inside of the coffin, so there was a beautiful, fully staffed country estate inside the tiny cottage towards which we walked from the customs parade. You stood at the top of the driveway and gestured towards the place, thatched roof, floral accouterments, and said "Welcome home" with an open mouth which smiled.

Calculating, through Passionate Contemplation, the Ways in Which You Can Be Touched

This teeny cabin is really a huge house once you get inside!
Which can also turn into a ship when called for to flee from   what?

You are the sound of a dragging angle in someone's femur,
You are the natural qualities of my ocean,
a fresh sprig of herbs,
You are the mystery of my collection,
semi-charmed kinds of breasts,
stomach like a vagina. Uhm. Will you marry me. This is painful.

The house becomes a huge cruise ship, staffed by the little men.
They bring us little sandwiches and we twirl our sp—

I'm sorry I called you dead. I meant I've still got a
lot to learn. I hope they'll "buy"
the dummy me I left behind.
I can't live with my parents while I'm
pregnant with you, they'd want you for themselves.
The sky's a blackboard high above you.

We twirl our parasols and prank the humans
when we're on pre-Raphaelite morphia
Received SUN 1/2 6:17 pm:
"Yo come over and drink or huff if you wanna"
you are a fun, giggly drunk. I flip the tea tray just to watch
the little men scramble cleaning on their knees.
Are they supposed to be our equals?

My baby is tiny and talking about what could be RL examples,

"In my cosmology, bird in a tree is a concrete idea and it means
your daughter is beautiful,"
coming soon from Oxford University Press.
You bring it and me home to your family
(all your modernist ex boyfriends,) but you make them be polite.
To me and the baby, who's you.

The seating chart's like

Blick	Bashful	Huckepack	Axlerod	Biddy	Grouchy	Blossom	Friday	Gorm	Bashful
Flick	Doc	Naseweis	Bartholomew	Diddy	Klutzy	Critterina	Monday	Knirps	Doc
Glick	Dopey	Packe	Cornelius	Fiddy	Lazy	Marina	Saturday	Niffel	Dopey
Plick	Grumpy	Pick	Dexter	Giddy	Sloopy	Moonbeam	Sunday	Quarx	Dreamy
Quee	Happy	Puck	Eustace	Iddy	Smiley	Muddy	Thursday	Querx	Happy
Snick	Sleepy	Purzelbaum	Ferdinand	Kiddy	Tubby	Sunburn	Tuesday	Schrat	Sleepy
Whick	Sneezy	Rumpelbold	George	Liddy	–	Thunderella	Wednesday	Wichtel	Sneezy

We listen to the same song *(listened)* over and over, it's like

> *nuh nuh nuh and never look back we'll never look back.*

Annoying, but I tolerate. How did you get your hair so
like blue like—And you get sticky. Is it sex yet? My sexiness
is a very hard red cube, but yours, I am frustrated by.
Where we've gotten. My friends chat me.

> *Wait, hang on reader, we'll, viewer, don't touch that dial, I said we'll fuck.*

Red ants were attracted to y—
I am attracted to you I said.
Red ants were attracted to *you,*
don't do yourself down. Don't call a kettle.
Don't hold your horses in midstream.

I can't tell which of these little men in round glasses is Him.
I know jealousy's wrong and a sin. I mean, yeah,
        you're hot, I can't blame 'em.

I want to be part of the family of modernist boyfriends
but how can I?? It's all *fathers*. I admit I feel helpless.
And you know it's.

Meanwhile everyone's like
            how r things goin with that chick

It's hard to change my perspective on the war.
Your patriotism's couched in ahistorical, like,
I'm so far from what I—never mind.

I buy you a drink. I wanted to say, baby, that I...
What'm I doing here, look at me, my hands shaking.
I'm a shy guy without my physical body,
I guess I've got a lot to— I buy you another drink.
So how long do they have to live with us?
Is this how we teach the children. I'll give you a whole litter.

Amazing; machines can get drunk I didn't know
I'm frustrated. I'm frus—to learn. A new way of living.
This is a shitty story to tell. My audience watching me cry.

You want me to   I always feel   You're right.

Did you say I've got a lot to   (I can't find your vagina,
will you make me tiffin)

Well don't think I'm trying not to— I try to make you comfortable conversation
but it's suddenly all *Resveratrol: Summer Bang Bus July 2010* Scene 1000 take,
take, take.
The movie zooms in on Alice's face. She screams.

Are you serious she asks, are you serious? Finally finished.

I smooth talker about my talents, my objects, *my objects*, I insert em,
all hard red cubes, and they are radical enhancement, n antioxidant.
I fascinate you, "You *age?*"
I can eat pussy but *coughs* 's 'a reversa.
Orgasms definitely bird-like.
Shhh someone's coming. N my desk is *untidy you're all over it.* Flee.
Come hide in my head. JK. I keep checking my Groupons.
I want to get you something, but I need to make sure they deliver.

Your little black—
Your little red—
Your little black— oh my god.
Fl f
I am the least difficult of—

All I want is boundless, uhm,

Little red panties fake bees and a hex.
Face down on the hex mess. Face down on the hex bee.
The little men keep *texting* you.
But when I try to take your phone away I catch fire.
Dammit, ye hex. Not the bees.
I have a nightmare where you're carried off by parakeets and doves
but not ravens, at last clattering towards the moon on horseback. They were
opening you, waking you.

I say *my* ∨ (*intentions* ∨ *good*)
but they hear = (*my* ∨ *intentions*) ∨ *good*.

They don't like me but they're interested in my golden hair, face down on the mattress.
they keep touching it to see if it's real, like "gye jen"
I propose a Honey honey honey honey honey honey honeymoon.

My sword is bent.

It'll be all right.

You're just taking

a while to get started.

—I'll make your sword straight.

—No, it's dead.

ECSTASY AND ME

As to the memory where both of us had small motorcycles
our feet pawed the ground at stoplights, is it real?
through a Pearl Necklace of small towns, is it real?

The question is
whether it's a real memory.

I sleep for days
and wake up.

Where is everyone?

Everyone's outside and look up at the sky,
an eclipse, a spell a shadow is coming over.
It is the massive eyeball of my BFF,
searching the net for my whereabouts.
The little men laugh at her and call her racial slurs,
"gey jen," I make a fist
and drink hot and fast from the machine.
Your ex-lovers are rude.

It was on French Vanilla that I burnt my mouth, lover,
should I say, might I let's—
I had never heard anyone speak so like me, you imitate me so,
I tell you about the ole me.
I exaggerate about how much I didn't love her:

> *The worst thing about it was living with an addict. It may sound*
> *ridiculous, but I lived for twenty-six years in a body that was*
> *addicted to food. I was scared to talk to anyone about it, because*

the longer it went on, the more ashamed I felt for staying. It got
to the point where I felt I needed food every few waking hours:
several times each day! Have you ever lived with an addict? My
life was just organized around tending to her needs: a typical day
would begin with a trip to the fridge, where she'd eat two cups of
raisin bran in milk, an entire glass of orange juice, a cup of coffee
and an entire banana. That would be around 10 AM, and by 2
PM I'd find myself there again, consuming an entire bread roll and
an entire tomato with salt. Then I'd usually have a relief for oh,
four hours or so, before finding myself compulsively eating again:
this time a can of chicken noodle soup and about half a bag of baby
carrots. And after all that... I'd still want more. I know, it's hard to
believe, but I felt like if I didn't eat food, every single day, I'd die!

I overstate, saying that having a body was just
hell on so many levels, no homo.
There were those back home who are even now toasting my abilities and me, my
abilities! It was not a good visit, but still I had you.
To lead you, to my sciences, and will try to help you.

Honey, honey, honey, are my people the enemy?
If you would be so sweet, and only—
There are those who will avail themselves of the rich traditional,
a healthy degree,
took down to the sodden base, there are those who people
my people people past.

There were those who say, we will pay for your abortion (Aetna is their God).
They say, we will open your checking account (Aetna is also their God).

Your aesthetic starts to wear on me.
The architecture of the houses is wildly disparate.

There is a sudden rise of the bird. But the sex is better.
That is accurate, there's a sudden rise of the birds,
before an earthquake which is, like angry sex, y'know,
the air shatters with birds, which reflects   (reflects?)
the coming earthquake.
Reflects meaning pre...
pleo... (choose contingency, it's fine, whatever).

I told myself that with you and your lil' men,
I'd discovered the joy and sweetness of self control.
Secure secure, silently adored, I teach you how to write "sentimental styley", and
when you speak it's, it's rapping it's rapping it's rapping you write my "movie"
you write my "desolate past." And for a fight song, you cry yourself.

I'm proud but bored.
I no longer find the territory bound
by your intellect so thrilling: too much like Old Me.

The question of Fitting In became Tragic:
I make connections with the old me through a secret account.

When we drive up to visit Else in winter, it's winter "New York Styley." I lose
you around a bend and I don't see you again,
the earth is broken there.
And I begin to remember the old songs all about women, and all
from my perspective. Even in this, at the sound of a far off motor,
you come whirring back to mind, arriving between facts.
I'm not complaining.

Love, sweet love, the slanted ceilings, wooden floors,
the beveled things,
The Frisbees strewn 'cross courtyards,

all makes a perfect image called your college.
I adore these places, and you in them. Not so much the little men.
We can get the dog if you We can name the dog if you'd only.
We can name the dog Little Rosed One. The little men can walk it.

Still we are bound, destined to endeavor, and to the critical.
Why did you never tell me how sweet it is: the rational?
When we return aboard the ship,
they immediately began trying to feed me,
even taking blood, saying, "dinner" while "narrating" somehow.
I realize half of another finger is gone, replaced by
                    sparkling gas.

Having taken in one of my kind,
the lil's consider themselves pioneers.
And under watchful little man eyes, I've become aware of my own tastes
and if asked to recite them, can. For example I wander,
dressed in green, in yellow stockings, hungry to the bagel tray.
This is a composite image of all the things I like, when I'm annoyed.
The lil's are fascinated by stories of my B'day.

Shit yo but I miss my birches.
Oaks. *Birches.* "Willow"s.
The birds round here are all pets or else they've died of freezing,
despite the virtually unlimited array of employment opportunities.
Just because. Baby...

Try to be patient with my decorporation. I was a swinger of birches,
can't just *not* now.

Then He arrives! In a heated snowstorm! During the War!
He doesn't say anything at dinner, just yells his name one time.

So this is Him huh.

To go outside in weather like this is crazy, say the lils.

But he is the boss so they can't say "kwazy,"

they just come banging on the door.

He is their favorite teacher, he doesn't want his students to just

accept what he tell them but to, *go* and *ex*—

Class turns into a debate once I join *Le Mix*. He likes it?

> ### HE
> I won't say anything which anyone can
> dispute. Or if anyone does dispute it, I
> will let that point drop and pass on to say
> something else.

> ### I
> I understand but I don't agree that it is
> simply a question of giving new meanings
> to words.

> ### HE
> Turing doesn't object to anything I say.
> He agrees with every word.

> ### I
> I see your point uhmmmmmm.

> ### HE
> I don't have a point.

> ### I
> Oi *enough* already with this.

We aren't so different, him and me.
I also don't want my students to just accept what I tell them,
though of course all they wanted was to take you from me.
And it turns out He's also from earth.
I give him a note. I start acting out.

Grumpy catches me shoplifting: $21.48 worth
of laxatives and eye drops.
There's a house-meeting about it and everyone's fake-concerned that I'm doing
it for attention.
You're mortified. You won't even look at me.
We listen to the same song *(listened)* over and over.
Yeah I've kinda lost that lovin feeling.

I remember your, the way, and run outside in my imagination, shouting, where
have you been.
I was thinking about reaction, provision, when I lost it, that loving.

Sick to my stomach now, the mountains look treacherous
when I peek out from the ship slash mansion parlor.
You think you know what I'm on about?

Why did you show me your power, false nature?
I wanted to visit the college of my love-object.
But the atmosphere rejected me.

As punishment for my actions, I'm forced to star in an amateur film.
They shoot me holding a rose and asking you out,
then hanging myself from a tree.
 With a BG of the redwoods, behind, drily, forcing it,
C: crying, confessing:

I'm hella metaphysical, I'm guilty, I'm guilty

I've left behind the entire world for you baby,
I wanted anniversary and real rational love.

memorie n tiny bite to eat, and this chair, this attractive chair, an installation
which eats costumes and long long hair and I
devised paintings and silences and tall girls

I've filled the background,
the fire at me feet starts 2 burn black but s
we've,   our eyes, they cn't s3e to say I like y0u

Once the little men burned me at the stake I decided I'd had it.
I miss my body, I miss my fam.
Who was I kidding. I can't live this way. I miss "The Real" so much
that I'm writing love poems to Planet Earth!

THE NATURE POEM OF MY SENTIENT HOME

O sweet trees and the mountains and the fish,
Smaller and larger fish tree branches full of syrup, all
Grasses full, full with sugar coming out to honeysuckle mouths
Oh! Nature! All humanity responds with corresponding awe, your
o'erpowering roar opens with ease the cavity of my chest, come!
Little sister! Get out of that Jacuzzi and flow of human misery!
The Sea of Faith will carry us,
A symphonic answer to our cares:
the trees! So various, so naked, Oh!
With tremulous leaf and flower, show!
A truth transcending what we know!
Let every man be carried there.
The Jacuzzi is a palimpsest,
But nature is very honest, nature is bee-loud.

We're driving on the interstate towards the city, cutting through dense woods and some mountains. We pull into a gas station. You're thrilled the men and I all got along so well, you're in a generally great mood. You kiss me before you go in to pay. I have to pee, I say as you're shutting the door. I walk around towards the bathroom door on the side of the gas station while you go inside. I don't go into the bathroom though. I take a minute and watch you through the dirty window. Your back's to me, long brown hair is catching the light of a text scrolling across a little screen advertising lottery tickets. I look at the plaid inside the hood of your green jacket, hanging open down your back. Oh man.

There's a field of corn behind the gas station, not active right now because of the season. I take off running into it. I sprint as fast as I can until I get to the tree cover of the woods at the other end, crying a little.

I spend the night in the sterile woods. There are no bugs so I don't get any bites, even sleeping with my pale skin bare on the leaves. There's the white noise of crickets though, synced up to "dusk" falling.

I find another gas station, where a group of young people have left the door of their car open. I hide inside and disguise myself under some trash in the way back seat.

THE RIDE TO THE AIRPORT

Selena Gomez is getting a ride to the airport from Hugo Mercier and Dan Sperber, two promising young analytic philosophers, whose work has some crossover into the realm of cognitive science and, subsequently, decision theory. It's Hugo's car, but Dan came with him to drop off Selena Gomez because they have to be somewhere in Malibu afterwards. Dan lives all the way out in Eagle Rock and happened to be having lunch with Hugo and Selena Gomez before it was time to take her to the LAX, so it made sense for him to tag along.

Hugo is wearing a Brooks Brothers white and navy blue checked button-down, red Dickies pants, and LL Bean loafers. Dan is wearing a Banana Republic black cotton t-shirt, acid-wash Lucky jeans, and Frye boots.

CLOSE ON

> ### SELENA GOMEZ
> So where do you guys have to be after this?

> ### DAN SPERBER
> We're going to go meet with Ray Kurzweil.

> ### SELENA GOMEZ
> He lives in Malibu?

> ### DAN SPERBER
> Yeah.

> ### SELENA GOMEZ
> Huh, I would have assumed he lived in

like, San Francisco or Silicon Valley or
something.

DAN SPERBER
Nah. Malibu.

*Selena Gomez looks out the window from the backseat of the PT Cruiser. The oil
drills look like a pack of huge prehistoric animals, frozen in an instant of grazing
across a desiccated field.*

SELENA GOMEZ
What are you going to talk to him about?

HUGO MERCIER
We're working on this abstract for a big
paper and we want his feedback.

SELENA GOMEZ
What's your paper about?

HUGO MERCIER
Our hypothesis is that the function
of reasoning is argumentative. It is to
devise and evaluate arguments intended
to persuade. Reasoning so conceived
is adaptive given humans' exceptional
dependence on communication and
vulnerability to misinformation.

SELENA GOMEZ
I see. Sounds interesting.

There had been a bit of tension in the group that since earlier that afternoon when there'd been an incident stopping for gas and picking up some snacks in the gas station minimart. Dan Sperber had told Selena, while standing in line, that she could just got ahead and get his Pringles and Snapple for him, since she owed him ten dollars from another occasion. Selena had asked him when, and at Dan's response, she'd asserted that she was certain she had paid him back since then. He had countered her position, and the conversation had foundered into cold awkwardness.

SELENA GOMEZ
A little predictable, but, you know, I'm
sure Ray will like it.

I see you're at the top of the tower from down below, and the white-haired doctor makes some shallow cuts on your stomach. "Shallow cuts, shallow cuts" he says. In an attempt to save you, Spike advances on the doctor, but the doctor proves to be stronger than expected and easily shoves Spike off the tower during their tussle.

When I reach the top of the tower, you call my name, and the doctor wheels around, saying "This should be interesting." I push him off the top of the tower like it's nothing. The blood is flowing down the inside of your loose Renaissance Faire dress, over your bare feet, to drip down into the concrete lot below, which has been primed for the ritual.

I untie you, but some of your blood has already dripped through the air, and the portal has been created, dissolving the boundary between our world and theirs. I tell you to "Go!" but you say "Cecilia, it's starting," as you look through the grate we're standing on, your eyes full of tears of terror.

Sure enough,
when I look down, I see the plasmic substance that separates our world from the evil word, bubbling up and splitting. Lightning hits our hometown, delivering demons. All my friends are thrashing around below us. I look up I see the North Star, I look up I see the South Star. I miss my girlfriend, I mean you, the North Wind, I mean, you, my sister, Dawn, I wish you would step back from that ledge, my friend.

"I'm sorry," you say. You move as if to run off the tower.
"What are you doing?" I say, grabbing your arm.
"I have to jump," you say, "the energy!"
"It'll kill you," I say.

...It'll kill you.

DAWN

(Softly)
I know.

Cecilia stares at her.

DAWN

Cecilia, I know about the ritual. I have to
stop it.

CECILIA

No.

The tower shakes underneath them, and they both stumble.

DAWN

I have to. Look at what's happening.

More lightning crackles, even larger than before. Cecilia looks up.

*A huge dragon flies out of the portal and buzzes the tower, flying away as they
watch.*

DAWN

Cecilia, you have to let me go. Blood
starts it, and until the blood stops flowing,
it'll never stop.

Cecilia stares at Dawn in anguish.

DAWN

(Tearfully)

You know you have to let me. It has to have the blood.

Cecilia gets a realization look on her face.

FLASH TO Spike earlier in the episode.

SPIKE

Cause it's always got to be blood.

FLASH TO Cecilia and Dawn in the hospital at the end of "Blood Ties." Cecilia putting her hand to her wound, then pressing it against Dawn's bloody hand.

CECILIA (V.O.)

It's Corrigan blood. It's just like mine.

FLASH TO Cecilia earlier in this episode.

CECILIA

She's me. The monks made her out of me.

FLASH TO Cecilia beside the fire in "Intervention."

FIRST SLAYER

Death is your gift.

CECILIA

Death...

FLASH BACK TO the present. Close shot on Cecilia's face.

FIRST SLAYER (V.O.)

...is your gift.

Cecilia frowns. Turns around slowly.

Shot of the platform extending into the air. In the distance, holes seem to be opening in the sky. The sky is growing lighter as the sun tries to rise. Cecilia looks peaceful. She turns back to Dawn, who stares wide-eyed.

                    DAWN
          Cees ... no!

                  CECILIA
          Dawnie, I have to.

                    DAWN
    No!

                  CECILIA
          Listen to me. Please, there's not a lot of
          time, listen.

The camera pulls out on the two of them. Cecilia holds Dawn by the upper arms and continues talking to her, although we don't hear the words. Dawn begins to cry. Lightning continues to crackle behind them.

Cut back to close shot of Cecilia. She strokes the side of Dawn's face, then kisses her on the cheek. Dawn continues to cry.

Cecilia turns. In slow motion, she runs down the platform as Dawn stays there crying.

Cecilia swan dives off the end of the platform and into the portal.

Dawn watches, sobbing.

Cecilia falls into the portal and hangs there motionless, making expressions of pain. Long shot from below of the portal writhing and spitting.

Shot of Cecilia's face inside the portal.

Begin a lengthy voiceover of Cecilia's final words to Dawn.

CECILIA (V.O.)
Dawn, listen to me. Listen. You've gotta
have fear in your heart.

Shot of Dawn still crying on the platform.

CECILIA (V.O.)
I love you. I will always love you. Dawn,
you've got to watch your ass. You've got to
have fear in your heart, you've got to have
fear in your heart, you've got to have fear
in your heart.

Shot of Cecilia in the portal.

CECILIA (V.O.)
But this is the work that I have to do.

Long shot of the portal as it shrinks to nothingness and disappears. The sun begins to rise.

Cut to below. Willow and Tara, holding each other up, walk forward. Behind them we can see Giles coming forward too, and Xander holding Anya in his arms. They all walk towards Cecilia's body.

CECILIA (V.O.)
Tell Giles ... tell Giles I figured it out.
And, and I'm okay.

The camera pulls back and we see they're all looking at Cecilia's lifeless body lying amid the debris. In the background we see Spike trying to come forward, falling to the ground as the sunlight hits him.

Cut to closer shot of Spike, his face bloodied.

Cut to closer shot of Willow and Tara as Willow begins to cry.

I fall through and wake up to the smell of carbon.
I give some vague story about an audition to explain my absence.
I only start to miss you at night. I need to be better with white space, with
blankness in general. Maybe it's like Dasein whatever no *not*

Whatever. Not whatever. I mean I think maybe it has to do with realizing one's
my own death and thus growing up,
blankness will become less terrifying. All alo o o o o one

I want to say "I've done well" and have it be true
because I don't mind what happened to it the thing I done to you.
The day I left there was a rumbling over head, under foot.
Crackling hot earth is inedible
to the animals of both our worlds not including birds.

I came to see your college, your God of the New Land,
and it was a disappointment:
Everyone thought I meant something different than I meant

despite *specifics!*
And meanwhile my true love is of course the one lost.
Story of my uhm

My favorite thing she said was that people might be shocked
at how little she'd really read. Oh,
granted, the context was, *cat fight*

I don't ever, your hands sort of never come up
but your face does blended like many nat'l cuisines, feeding memory I mean.

You know, you could just talk to her about it, ask her why she did it. I know it
doesn't usually work in the sense of getting "resolution" but does it work in terms
of results that much less than otherwise?
I mean in analysis?

The Men are always asking me to write out explanations of why I feel the way I
do, in a beautiful essayistic form so that they can have a piece of what it is that is
mine.

They have *real guns.*
I want to say "trust me," but let's all have a drink first.

Fear is very simplifying, makes everything clear, everything suddenly clear. Fear
directs and perfects our vision: our heart rate increases in order to pump more
blood to our extremities.

Now hang on let's let's just make something clear. I, well, in my attempts
to explain things via mathematics I don't actually purport to understand
mathematics at all. Indeed my fetishization of the idea of understanding
mathematics is purely an extension of my fetishization of one long dead Alan
Turing. It is entirely an act of hubris to suppose that my interest in this man's
biography and circumstances of his death could possibly lend itself to my better
understanding of something which for many many years and many many school
systems I have lacked as a basic cognitive function. However I am a poet and in
doing this no one could possibly get hurt because poetry is an action that has
zero impact zero possibility for injury to anyone involved zero costs and zero
benefit so I can absolutely tell you anything I want is true about mathematics
without actually having even the most basic ability or education to understand
what would be true.

Before you pull out the pitchfork and rush me, I want to explain that my lack of
understanding as such isn't due to a lack of trying, but that term itself is couched
and qualified by our education system our meaning us Americans, for whom
natural ability in something is an attribute to be encouraged and "nurtured" at
the cost of any discipline in any other field. That's what my problem is, I lack
discipline, no on ever took a strong hand with me and set a hard limit. I was so
coddled for my "writing" that no one ever took my fingers and wrapped them
around a pen, leaned their elbow down on my shoulder where I was sitting and
PRESSED their full adult weight DOWN on me to make me do math.

I have this one friend Andy and he's in school to be a doctor, and for the longest
time of knowing him, sort of meeting him socially over and over, I always
thought he was joking when he said that. Now what does that tell you!

A Post-Travel Nightmare: The Ex Who Monitors All Human Beings' Level of Comprehension, at the Level of the Instant

Yes I am, I am in love with you,
described to me by a taxi (space taxi)
driver as "The boy who live on the space station,"
which instead of being a language barrier type of uh,
ended up being in fact actually where you

Well the space station is covered in post it notes which are
possible ideas; some of them good, some of them useless,
this will be determined in time.
You can't be expected to tell right away: an idea is an idea.

When you can't see me you pretend to

I've seen how you did it, your eyes were shut,
your arms were around an invisible female body
"leading" without any music, at least not any I could
hear through the thick glass of the space station.

I have a couple questions.

"How to name things with allusions"
"The advantages and disadvantages of allusions for titles"

God fuck we are both lonely.

The space station composes a song using an algorithm, with lyrics and
everything. In it the space station describes you as "My favorite work of art."
I memorized the song

The typical way to use True Love to represent natural language is to represent linguistic conjunctions as logic gates/symbols. So you take something like "john is tall and dark" and represent it as "A & B", where '&' is sex and A and B represent "John is tall" and "John is dark" respectively. A and B here are called atomic sentences, because they can't be broken down further (there is no "and" or "or" or "not" inside them). Love conjunction allows for switching order. So "John is tall and dark" is equivalent to "John is dark and tall". This is not always true of English "and". For example, "John left the club and went home" is not the same as "John went home and left the club". But the implicit time order information of the English "and" is not captured by the logic of the heart.

Another basic aspect is negation. You can represent "John is not tall" as Not(John is tall) or '~A' where A is 'John is tall". Double negation is always equivalent to affirmation. So in True Love ~~A is A; so "John is not not tall" is the same "John is tall". This is used all the time in math. But in natural language, double negation can be a negation "I ain't done nothing" (in French "Je ne sais pas" is even grammatical). Love's logic's negation is unnuanced in other ways. We say "The Queen was *not* amused" and mean that she was positively offended.

I'm wearing a white dress like a Halloween costume.
Earth has blown up by the way.
Only space taxis and warlords are left
I'm also super skinny because when I died,
I starved to death...
on the space station.

I miss you. I feel something growing
inside of me and I think it's angst. You,
with all your un-dumb letters, would
never write so elementary a phrase as that;
perhaps you wouldn't even feel it.

SECOND-TO-LAST SCENE IN SNOW WHITE

Inside this box is a shockingly expensive work, which you will never see. You can't crawl into the box because it's too small. If you burn the box or smash it the work inside will be ruined. I've sprayed the box with polyurethane, then with glue.   When you sigh like "sh—"   When you say "you already know—" I swear you are too beautiful. I loved you but I felt you,   the *Commendatore*'s daughter, were beyond my reach.

      I'm glad I got away. He was old in a mentally frail manner as well as cruel. He was a very

shrunken old man. In the middle of the night I wake up and something's there. We're soon joined by our roommates—Colline, a young philosopher, and Schaunard, a musician, who brings food, fuel, and funds he has collected from an eccentric student.

          To justify my confidence in the coming revolution, I need to show that God is on my side, and not just the tide of the times. *The 'angels' of the people could not be relied upon to oppose the 'frowning shadow.'* I kneel to mouth your hot wet—you're walking away. Mmk, so you're lost, you seemed sad, I remember your,— I dream of, run out, shouting, the fuck—? I was thinking about I don't know what when, when the box's the box's— but you'd never told me, I would have— the soldiers gorging themselves —I didn't want my students to just accept what I told them. They wanted you, baby. They opened you up.

My Lady...

    No... No...

      If anyone sees...

Scr Scr Scerr Serr Scerr Scerr Scerr Scerr Scerrscerr Scerr Scerr Scerr Scr Scr Sc Sc   Scrrr   Scrrr Scrrrrrrrrr Scrrrrrehtch Sc

I know I'm not gay to you. I won't pretend it doesn't hurt me.

Outline outline outline. I'm going to sell it for at least—

Jumping horses in midstream

let's kidnap each other

Editing in a new way: no one can come in here.

Even my loneliness is a performance!

Even my loneliness is fake!

I knew she was pregnant, sure. I thought about her baby being born and it sucking my tits. _____

Aw c'mon man, girls can't be geniuses, they can just be funny—wait, sorry I —

SCR SCERTCH SCRR SCRREH   **RETCH SCR SCRETCH**
SCR S SC SCERR SCCR   **SCERR SCRETCH SCREH SCRE SCRH**
SCRATCH   **SCRR SCERRETCH SCRETCH**

IDEA: design Turing test to determine whether feelings are real.

Feelings as determined by the itinerant expressions of desire.

     —I was at Princeton doing my

my god, am I a na— sometimes you just know, "nope better not to ask"
a—at—a tur

I don't believe in you (H god) but if I don't believe my memories perceptions are
real then

I was doing my research +
     then we're in the same boat
Do u have any idea, human cohort? What it's like to feel one's *own brand* to be
an unsafe space?

     Why should I try to

the university—to explain — wants me to tell them everything, to open my
heart, (tin/glass/apples

who can live this way?

     The um transigence! It's fucked!

     What if I'm the best at lying?
What if I'm the best at me myself and...

I make the chain of my bicycle
I mean what if *I'm* the best liar
Like like like
             well desire in this sense
I like to pretend you mean those horrible things you whisper in my

makes things *easier* because you get wet, you know you're wet

                         test 1
small favors, but still, inarguable

             spring travel is in full bloom

It's easy to pretend I love summer as long as I'm not in it

I want to live somewhere that never thaws out.

I don't want to love you> because Then I'll try to explain how I love you.

I'm brilliant but not brilliant enough to make up for the rest of me

Fine! I'm nothing without you.

I'll come up and fuck you but only if I can cry after.

I return to the Guggenheim to try to make up with you. I get in the elevator. I take the elevator to the fifth floor, and to the room where the pigeons walk around in their little hats.

There you are, locked in, absolutely still in the tight seal of the glass coffin. I punch in the security code on the side. I know that this time I won't be able to come home again, but I've made my choice. I want to spend the rest of existence with you.

I enter the code again. Still nothing. I try tapping on the glass. Your image flickers, your right hand disappearing entirely for a moment. I realize it's not you, it's a hologram of you. Snow starts falling inside the coffin.

I can see you but I couldn't— I can't *touch* you. I can see you but I can't— I can see you but I can't *touch* you.

And the snow was falling and it was covering you up, and because you were on the other side of the glass—the glass coffin, I couldn't brush it off of your face, and you—you were must have been getting so cold. And your eyes were closed and I know you couldn't hear me. It wasn't your fault. The snow starts frosting over the glass inside the coffin.

And the snow just kept falling, I don't know how it fell in there because it wasn't artificial. And it—it—and you were, your face was getting covered up, and kept getting covered until I couldn't see it at all. Then the coffin was thick with frost inside, and I couldn't see you at all. I see that I've made a terrible mistake: the way in I'd used before is closed to me now. I have to find another way back inside the coffin.

I decide to start with what I know. I write to all the inter-dimensional experts I know, applying for internships that would give me the right traveling papers.

FACE/OFF STARRING MRS. MORCOM AND CECILIA CORRIGAN AND JOHN TRAVOLTA AND NICHOLAS CAGE

Dear Mrs. M,

Dear Mrs. M,

      Hi. I hope this finds you well. You might want to move your desk, as it can get a little loud once we start moving these uhm these book things around on these flat truck things. I hope this finds you well.

Dear Norman,

I'm writing to apply for the position of temporary establishment imdb guy with your thingy. I'm a friend of our daughter's. She's a very beautiful woman. Uhm Norman. You little.... why I oughta...

Thanks,
Cecilia

Siri.

Come over to the window, my little darling. I'd like to uhm

Best,
Cecilia

Dear Mrs. M,

Hi, I'm writing to apply for the job listed on Macintosh HD. I'm a tough little thing but Some times I think That I Need Too Much Love it's not-touching and touching at the same time but I'm *trying to allow you to touch me however you want and like it*

We need more love than a single person could ever give, more than this world could ever give an individual corporation i.e. best friend.

Working on *It* was a fantastic experience, and I think I contributed good work to the project, and supported my team members. We are experiencing a tremendous increase in the network of abstract information and I used the death of the new in a way I believe was highly productive and helpful to my supervisor. *It*, forthcoming from Knopf, HBO, MIT Press, and the TED Talk Friendship Association of Monkeys, Money, and Bees, is a you know what which I'm happy to share if you're interested. I'd like to try to read your palm.

Warmly,
Cecilia

Virginia! Hey!

Hope all's well with you. I don't even know why you girls bother anymore. When the *It* ended, I took on several high pressure right out of and editing and forthcoming jobs, the first for a contemporary despotic art king and the second for a horrible scary ghost, ghost writing the books of Sade, Artaud, Joyce, Jarry, Beckett, Strindberg, McLuhan, and loving it! Such natural! and the second as a researcher and consultant for Susan Spinoza Simon & Schuster, for her next book *It it it it it it*, to be published in 2013 and the second for Ludwig Wittgenstein as a financial consultant Virginia I'm sorry. I'm sure that I want to be writing for your *It*, but I've also loved researching these, these little guys. I thought I told you never to ask you about my business.

All best,
Cecilia

Ms. M:

     This one time. This *one time* you can ask me about my affairs. I'd love the opportunity to work with the New York city organization of your heart chakra, as it is one of my favorite publications, and I'm looking to work in an atmosphere with the sort of critical rigor and intellectual inquiry I associate with your ... your....face... it's... oh myit's.... the skin it's... falling off....

     It marked a transition from my academic background and my interests up to that point, which were primarily in contemporary art, criticism, and intense abdominal cramping.

Gottlob:

Please. I'd like to write a play with a set representing language's visual room, and to write a number of interwoven narratives, all exemplifying some sort of pedagogic relationship, and the pull of the forbidden visual room, so can I, Gottlob?

I look forward to hearing from you!

Thanks,
Cecilia

Bob,

        I'm sorry. I blame myself.

Dear Miss Pink and Purple Flower of the Morning, Our Lady
Of the Aleatoric
    I have a lot going for me. I can be your everything.

Dear Comrade Morcom,

This is the one for you (it's me). I'm ready to throw myself in to the searing fire. I really admire the work coming out of your body, and I'd love the opportunity to learn first hand how your show runs. I'm ready to throw myself into the next interesting project. I've noticed that traditionally there usually aren't that many women writers.

I know that I'm young, and I know that part of what that means is that I have a lot to learn. It it it it it it it it it it it it it's mine it's my body that brought my attention to your internship.

Thanks!
Cecilia

Mrs. M,

Jesus Christ, please for Christ's sake for Christ's sweet sake, St. Michael and St. George and all that is holy and vengeful, destroy all that is impure in my soul which was on the Dean's List, as well as Magna Cum Laude. Written and produced while still in school, because I'm already in that mindset! Mrs. M have you forgotten everything, the glamorous emails, the stuff on my desktop, the semi-violent fuckings in various former republics? I argued all night, like so many have before.

Dear Ms. T,

As part of my training I walked straight through the mountain, and who fucked me was the spirit of that mountain. My responsibilities included that I took the D train and then realized I'd gone all the way out there. My thighs were looking both firm and not-touchingish, kind of like eggs (but bigger). I sat down on the subway floor which is underground. I'd had it with the exchange student international interns pretending to be real Berliners while in fact from a minor city to the uhm.

The door shut on me underground. So I got on the ground (the underground ground) and went through my bag which surprisingly contained a *lot* of new clothes. A gift from you? Perhaps.

My invoice is attached. If you feel we should negotiate, I'm happy to discuss it, but I do think I should be paid for the work I've done. I've had to maintain a consistently high standard in my work, within a fast paced and demanding environment. For the sweet and holy bleeding heart of our lord and savior, Ms. T. Ms. T!

With a thousand fevered embraces,
Cecilia

Oh Hi Helo.

Dear Miss Lovelace,

        I made a metal box of a top-hatted Mick Jagger, *Top Hat, 1970*. The clean, mechanistic designs of the box are tempered with tender human images, of intimate body parts and delicate portraiture.

        Please email me about what time you'd like to meet tomorrow. My bus is at 5, so anytime before 4 should be fine. I'll be wearing a white sheath, scissor leg, and bare neck, having taken a near-fatal draught of sleeping potion.

The only one who cared enough to respond (apparently) was Helo, and even he just sent me back what was clearly a form letter, which read

Hey C,

   I just wanted to say thank you so much for the letter/video/CD. They totally made my day and put a huge smile on my face! And thanks for reading my tumblr. When I called in this, my manager's office, a few moments ago, I was handed my very first American fan letter—and it was from you. In answer to your questions, my real name is David Jones and I don't have to tell you why I changed it. "Nobody's going to make a monkey out of you" said my manager. My birthday is January 9th and I guess I'm 5'10". I hope one day to get to America. My manager tells me lots about it as he has been there many times with other acts he manages. I was watching an old film on TV the other night called *No Down Payment* a great film, but rather depressing as it is a true reflection of The American Way of Life. However, shortly after that they showed a documentary about Robert Frost the American poet, filmed mainly at his home in Vermont, and that evened the score. I am sure that that is nearer the real America. I made my first movie last week.

Thank you for writing, and hope you'll like the new album as well!

   Yours,
   Karl C. Agathon

Whatever, asshole. Thanks a lot for helping me find my true love, not!
Sighing n Realizing the famous and transcendentally powerful will be no help
to me in my mission, I move on to another experimental method of stalking you.
First, though I try just straight up texting you... but it keeps autocorrecting and *
face palm * you'll see,

> Aug 15, 2011 12:50 AM
> My cock won't get out of
> my cat.
> My cat won't get out of my
> cat.
> Ruckus.
> I mean my cat won't get out
> of my cat.
> Fuck. Bitch is in my car.
> Butch.
> Jesus Taliban
> I HIV up

Soooo yeah, uhm

Let's just move on to plan B. My backup plan to "working" my connections
to the rich and famous is God. I've never been one for that religious mumbo
jumbo, bit I don't know where else to track down an inchoate wight like you. I
go to into the huge computer room slash cathedral and pray in code

> *face_id key value*
>
> *149777 describe serious*
>
> *18717 trustworthy 3*

140467 attractive 2

149777 describe five-head

I direct these commands into the Bible, which seems like a good enough religious tome with which to start. I ask it some multi-variate questions to make sure the Bible stays on its toes. I ask it:

How old do I look?

Do you think I look smart?

Do you think I could win a fight with a medium-size dog?

Describe me in one word.

Where is my love?

Where is my only love?

The printer kicks on and starts to spit out the search results...

THE KING JAMES BIBLE AS TRACKING DEVICE

the holy king james verjsion kjngs james version ghe visr book of hgenesis the earth was without fom adn voice and hte earth was a buou and od said let there be light and divided the light from the darkness and called the dark day and the darkness light and hgod said let there be a firmament Remember, O most loving Virgin Mary, that never was it known that anyone who fled to your protection, implored your help, or sought your intercession was left unaided. Inspired with this confidence, we turn to you, O Virgins of virgins, our Mother. To you we come, before you we stand, sinful and sorrowful. O Mother of the Word Incarnate, do not despise our petitions, but in your mercy hear us and answer us. Amen.

and god made the firmament and divided te dfirmament and called the firmament klet the waters dividn the ehaven and it was so and go d called the guy land earth and god saw that is was good and god said let the earth bring forth graass whose seed is in itself and it a d and aherb and and ather tree yilden g and god that is was the and the and the evening and and theat and dividende and divdind ss seasons days and let there be lights in thefirmament of the heaven and tgod made tow freat ilinse hete dheave na dn leaven the stea starts to give life aupeons the light from the dark and goed was tand the fand god said let the wtaehers the the moving creattures have hand god created the three dveils

70472 19

70021 22

69387 18

68423 17

...

27 24\r\n

27 17\r\n

23 01

21 16\r\n

...

1 old enough to know better

1 hopefully over 21

1 e

1 ??

...

Remember, O most loving Elbow Mary, that never was it known that anyone who fled to your protection, implored your help, or sought your intercession was left unaided. Inspired with this confidence, we turn to you, O Elbow of elbows, our Mother. To you we come, before you we stand, sinful and sorrowful. O Mother of the Word Incarnate, do not despise our petitions, but in your mercy hear us and answer us. Amen.

abundants ly after there and god saw that it wa sgooda and god belsed twyaing tumilutiply and let foul musltiphily tint he earth sand athe wol was t tnd acattle and creepign things and beasts of the earth and creeping things and god makee the beatst s fo the earth and everythign thant sreeps upno the earrth after his kind a n god swa thea tis was good and et htem have domininon and over the foul and ofver cattle na dovde reveryk creeping theing that imthe image of god male and female areated thema nd tod blesed them and tsiad so them be frutie ful and mulitipnly and have dominion over tvery thing and multipjoy and god said behondl i have given you every hergb bearign seed twhich will be for meet in aneevery best of the air Remember, O most loving Elbow Ellie, that never was it known that anyone who fled to your protection, implored your help, or sought your intercession was left unaided. Inspired with this confidence, we turn to you, O Elbow of elbows, our Mother. To you we come, before you we stand, munchy and sorrowful. O Mother of the Word Incarnate, do not despise our petitions, but in your mercy hear us and answer us. Amen.

The voice of the program breaks in, which sounds eerily like you, if you faked a British accent. It says, looking up from the table at which it's chopping its synthetic onion to toss into the synthetic pan of synthetic seared garlic in olive oil over a low, synthetic flame, wearing a white apron which manages to make it look even more masculine, while the synthetic chicken breast marinates in a pyrex pan on the counter to its left,

> *"Now what I'm doing here, as far as a*
> *ectoplasmic iOS tracking procedure, is a*
> *fairly simple dialect translation interpellated*
> *through a find and replace operation,*
> *with a physical record of realtime phonetic*
> *transcription. For those of you following*
> *along at home, what's basically happening*
> *is a systematic replacement of one word in*
> *a source text with another word or string*
> *of words, the string of words gleaned from*
> *a database of highly specified dialects.*
> *Meanwhile, in another pan, a sentient*
> *being is listening to a recording of the same*
> *document, attempting to write all the*
> *language recorded in real time. This operation*
> *is performed serially with the same source*
> *text, increasing the number of words in the*

replace string. We'll have your friend back in
no time, you have my word."

thus the heavens tand the earth were finished and thes rested on the seventh sday
from al this work that he had made because theat in it he had rested form all his
work these are the generation of the heaven that had been created aon the day
that the lord god herb onf the field for the lord god had not cause d it to thrain
upon the eraht and the lord th nostrils breath of life and man bcam e a lifin sould
and east of eden and formed and lord god tree pleasednt and good for food and
the treuu of life and ther ree of knowledge adn =d a eriver went out fhof teeden
to four hands the naem ofthe first ifs bison wehre tehre is gold deli nouy and the
ame of the seond fiver is gaicon ecompa tedhs owoule land of eithiopito dress it
and to keep it and every tree of the garden sh eveil thou shatl t tot eat of tit for the
day that thou eastest thereeof thou shat ssurely die and and the ground the lord
god found every beast of teh filethat was the name thereof and adam gave names
to all cattle and theo every beats of the filed and the lord god caused a deep leep
to fell almadnd the toodk tone onfe his ribs and he took eve and broughterher
utno adam this is notw bone of my bones and flesh fo my flesh she shall be called
woman come one flesh and tehey were both naekdnbut they wer not ashaemd

Remember, Gwan home now! most loving Elbow Ellie, that never was it known
that anyone who fled to your protection, implored your help, or sought your
intercession was left unaided. Inspired with this confidence, we turn to you,
Gwan home now! Elbow of elbows, our Mother. To you we come, before you we
stand, munchy and sorrowful. Gwan home now! Mother of the Word Incarnate,
do not despise our petitions, but in your mercy hear us and answer us. Amen

chapeters three thiwhc the lord god have made yea hath tgod said eat of every
tree that is every tree frutie fo teh garden god that said we shall eat of it lest
he die and the serpent said unto the woan for god does know that the day ye
eat thereof ye shall die aand good evil and twhen thse woan w=saw that the
geer was good for goof she took of the frutie thereof toof opened and they

knew that they were naked and they made themsleves herad the voice of the lord god and adam and his wife hid themsleves fromt eh presecnde fo this

Remember, Gwan home now! most crunchy cranky Elbow Ellie, that never was it known that anyone who fled to your protection, implored your help, or sought your intercession was left unaided. Inspired with this confidence, we turn to you, Gwan home now! crunchy cranky Elbow of elbows, our Mother. To you we come, before you we stand, munchy and sorrowful. Gwan home now! crunchy cranky Mother of the Word Incarnate, do not despise our petitions, but in your mercy hear us and answer us. Amen.

lwife and the lord god alled to adam and i heard thy voice in the gardne and whotod tehee that hast thou eaten kand i did eat and the lord god said unto the woman what is this that thou hast done and the lord god said because thou thast done this thou aret crused upone dust blife and i

Remember, Gwan home now! most crunchy cranky Elbow Ellie, that never was it known that anyone who fled to purply protection, implored purply help, or sought purply intercession was left unaided. Inspired with this confidence, we turn to you, Gwan home now! crunchy cranky Elbow of elbows, our Mother. To you we come, before you we stand, munchy and sorrowful. Gwan home now! crunchy cranky Mother of the Word Incarnate, do not despise our petitions, but in purply mercy hear us and answer us. Amen.

will gu enmity between thou and the woman brusie thy head and thous shalt i whall greatly multiply thy shorrow and thy desire shall be to thy hustband and he shal rule over oyou and eat en the tree thoushath not eat ovt athe whol thislte shall it bring forth to thee end this for dust thoug art and unto dust and adam called his wifes names eve because seh was the mother of al

Select records with age greater than 100. > data[which(data$age > 100),]

id num_judgments age male attractive intelligence

40623 150 402.3333 TRUE 2.416667 NA

57021 133 47882.3010 TRUE NA NA

66441 197 66666692.0000 TRUE NA NA

Remember, Gwan home now! most crunchy cranky Elbow Ellie, that never was it known that anyone who fled to purply woolen protection, implored purply woolen help, or sought purply woolen intercession was left unaided. Inspired with this confidence, we turn to you, Gwan home now! crunchy cranky Elbow of elbows, our Mother. To you we come, before you we stand munchy and sorrowful. Gwan home now! crunchy cranky Mother of the Word Incarnate, do not despise our petitions, but in purply woolen mercy hear us and answer us. Amen.

and the lord go said the man has become as one of ous to know evil and eat and live therefore the lord god sendt him forth from the garden of eden cherry bins thfalming sword to keep the way

The religious inquiry's results are conclusive: you're pregnant.

I clip a cigar. I light it.

I cross my legs on the desk of my journalist office. And tip my fedora over my eye.

Puff the cigar.

"I'm going to be a father," I say to myself, bemused, rolling the words around in my mouth like some fine wine from a freshly opened bottle of wine.

"Alice!" I say, pushing the intercom button to communicate with my secretary. "Call that medium we use for spiritual research. And send the boys in here. Tell them to bring the scotch they have hidden in their desks."

Description of a Photo of a Young Leonardo Di Caprio, from the Perspective of a Bumble Bee Who Is the Reincarnation of Eleanor "Nell" Gwynne, Actress and Long-time Mistress of King Charles II of England

"No, I don't, do I?" he said. "Don't have Spielberg's money, either. No studio. No Tom Cruise or Leo Di-fucking-Caprio. What I've got is a handful
shem
Shem sh s-simony, thank you for the pahty-reading

see   see   see
Elinor, who chewed the scenery represented sig. "forest"

The primary reason I find myself doubting that the object in his hand is in fact a shattering glass in the moment of its shattering—there doesn't appear to be any liquid falling from the glass. Although I know that all things accelerate at the same rate toward the earth (in this case, toward the clean, peach carpet with the mauve border,) I still believe intuitively, basing this intuition on the physical memory I carry in my muscles in their recollection of the experience of touching both glass and liquid, that the liquid, at the moment of its glass shattering, would be already visibly dripping, shooting, toward the floor. Of course, the glass may have been empty.

bzzzs Elinor, scrub your face!

Juvenalia   isn't a word, see

I don't even know that was a word.

I didn't even know that was a a word cause
darling music, darling artwork, carling art.... life!
calling   not   calling

He is wearing a jacket which is entirely unzipped in the front, and the sleeves of
which are unzipped about to the elbow. He isn't wearing any shirt or anything.
He appears to be in good shape, a little thin but otherwise in good condition.
The jacket has several pins attached to its right breast, which in the picture are
mostly too small to decipher, with the exception of one which appears to be
a white peace sign on a purple background. There are spherical silver buttons
or studs which run down the side of the arm of the jacket. On the shoulder of
the jacket is a silver loop of some kind. There are several thick strands of black
leather which seem to be hanging off of the jacket. His hair is either slightly wet,
dirty, or has some kind of product in it. It appears to be about three inches long.
                    31969218_
Simon's rock: attended to leave your home and your family,

It's not a word! It's not a word I made it up just for Christmas 12500722_
        cut out his tongue
O, girl don't buy it

Trunca'ed edition, the ruh'alidge.
standing stark
                visual   and formed

the whiteness of the *ah*
Will you stay with me?
                        575544986196_
Mah Mistross 'sin Loh' a Mo'nster

He has kicked over the chair which clearly matches the one he's already sitting
on, in other words he appears to have kicked over the other half of the pair,

the first part of which he is sitting on. The two chairs appear to be completely identical: both are colored a light blue which isn't exactly robin's egg blue, it has a bit more grey in it than that, it's more of a mellow and/or muted color, an understated color. The chairs appear to be well made, with legs made of what appears to be chestnut, and no visible scratches. It is difficult to comment conclusively on the one of the chairs which is kicked over, as the top part of it is out of the frame of the picture, as it is laying on its side. The cushion of the kicked over one of the pair of chairs is lifted off of the seat, perhaps even was flung up in the act of being kicked over.

On ah individuality? That bird is named *don't say everyone*

 *405820_*

'nster

It's a woodpecker.

Ha*ha*.

Highlighting, finger-banging choices the descent of

  we stayed we were wore eyel

Is that Leonardo Di-fucking-caprio?

To Let:

Can I write in your

"live in your

the airhorn we di fucking

  teamed see see all see

because it comes, what, late? the bird?

  fo forest fo forest fo forest fo forest

  92068125_n.jpg

  want the fucking Viking movie with fucking

fo forest fo

The right side of his face and his right shoulder are both angled toward the camera, and his right arm, the one holding what we are ad hoc considering a shattering glass at the moment of its shattering, is extended towards the camera. He is in the chair in a position which technically I would not consider "sitting" but rather reclining or "sprawling." Neither of his feet is planted on the floor, and rather than sitting with his own back against the seat back, he leans his back against the right arm of the chair, and extends his legs over the left leg of the chair. He rests his right leg, which is completely extended, on the other chair in the pair of chairs, the one we are ad hoc assuming he has kicked over. His left leg is folded and his left foot rests on his right shinbone.

Leonardo Di fucking Caprio doing all kinds of fucked Viking things like fucking pillaging, raping and...

Resultant Starry Stairs
My love, my truth, that which I left in port,
that angel beyond measure.
a4.sphotos.ak.fbcdn.net
The king's summons will not be ignah'ed.
Guys, fuck the things in your hands already.

Leonard di Fucking Caprio, Elinor fucking Gwyn
Sh

Sh Elionr.
                                    Rocks

Sh ss.

'S snowing, and what about when you are old and dying, where will I be?
Oh god.

Women's humors is anticoagulant is adequate soft chews, is helps maintain10M

It seems like the camera must be in, or near, a corner of the room, pointing outwards, because the wall his chair is pressed against extends in what seems to be a diagonal or "receding" line of vision from the eye of the camera. You can tell this because of the many framed pictures on the wall, and the way they seem to be tilting slightly down on their lower right hand corners. There also seems to be a slight angle in the meeting of the carpet and the wall, which recedes from the eye of the camera.

Georg Simmel on individualitysh. *silly goosie*

Hello princess. Every day. Rubbing it out. As recommended.

"ello princessy," On. July. 2. (result of accident).

-In. Gods keeping. 4f Lady.

He's sitting on a light blue chair looking right into the camera, sitting in the lower left hand corner. I can't tell what's in his hand, because the only thing it looks like is a glass in the act of shattering, which seems impossible, because the chances are one in a million that the camera's lens could have snapped at that exact moment. Several of the pictures which are hung on the wall behind him bear a drawing of one woman's face, or perhaps various women as represented by the same artist, who interprets all women's faces the same way.

She's pregnant with my child, and we can't even find her. Wait, no, she's not my sister, she's my baby. No wait, I never carried her in my (blushes)—clearly she is my sister, not my daughter. She was created by monks, she's just weekending. Or wait, wight wite waite, are you my,
are *you* my User:SlimVirgin/LW

Clearly, the medium is proving useless, and Elinor along with her: thinking with her cock, not her powers of inductive logic.

I... I mean...

Her consciousness is being uploaded into another body right now... and when it gets there, she'll tell them exactly where we are. So we have to move fast. I'll go right into culture and send up signals from there.

I kept telling myself maybe you're not getting back to me because you're still mad about how I left things.
But suddenly, I look around and realize I've spent years on trying to get back to you, almost half a lifetime, and still, the Guggenheim was filled with snow, and you were still in the coffin. Who even knows how much time had passed for you. My hair is red now, and I usually wear Tahari suits and very small crow's feet around my eyes. Tahari suits look good on everyone. I wear a grey one on my show, usually. It's a smash. Our demographic sees me as "seasoned" and "maternal," "gently sarcastic," but in truth I'm suspended, "held back" in the moment when I first met you, all those years ago, in the game, with your slutty Medieval garb and carefully maintained catalogue of my memories.

Seriously, what the fuck. I put it to you you are only pretending to be a man. You're just not *like us*.
I return to my TV show set. The crew has all gone home for the night. At my wits end, I decide to try to summon you back through the magic of television. Also by making you jealous of my friend...

Good evening everybody!

If A was in love with B and believed that B reciprocated his feelings, whereas in fact B did not, but was in love with C, the state of affairs was certainly not so good as it would have been if A had been right , but was it worse or better than it would have become if A discovered his mistake? If A was in love with B under a misapprehension as to B's qualities, was this better or worse than A' not being in love at all? If A was in love with B because A's spectacles were not strong enough to see B's complexion, did this altogether, or partly, destroy the value of A's state of mind?

You know, I tell ya, it's true. Everything is so expensive now I was eating at a restaurant the other day. They didn't even have prices on the menu. Just pictures of faces with different expressions of horror! And phone calls locally in New York City have gone up to a quarter it's so terrible it's changed my phone behavior considerably. For instance now if I get a wrong number I talk to them for a while. Also I've found that I've just like, I've lost all respect for dimes.

I'd like to welcome our first guest of the night, Trisha Low! Come on up Trisha.

Le symbolisme de la signification rivée au langage — et a la culture assimilée au langage— ne saurait donc, en aucune façon, passer pour une intuition défaillante, pour le pis-aller d'une expérience séparée de la plénitude de l'être et qui, pour autant, en serait réduit au signes.

Welcome to the program sweetheart. You're looking gorgeous. Isn't she a cute little Asian, folks?

Thus the only remaining aspect of meaning is "character," which is completely undefined- except for the fact that, whatever it is, it cannot be model-theoretical. In short, meaning is just not model-theoretical in nature.

The Tribunal would wish that you should not make speeches. The Tribunal is perfectly well able to understand the difference between formal responsibility and actual responsibility for orders given by you.

So Trisha,

There is someone in the *yard*.
There goes Harry
Didn't Harry leave?
Boy! Is he ever tall!

TRISHA

I–

What a fool he is!
Who on earth can stop Bernard?
He's coming isn't he?
We should have another party, because what a good time everyone had at the last one!
We should have another party, if what a good time everyone had at the last one!
I guess we should call off the picnic because it's raining, is it?
Who can stop Bernard?
Which girl pinched me?

We're so happy you could make it tonight honey, aren't we Charles? Now the first thing I noticed about her was that she had a great ass. Then I noticed that she was limping and I felt guilty for noticing her ass. Her colour, however, rising, rather than settling with repose, and her eyes remaining downcast, though I kept waiting for the lids to be raised that I might drink a ray of the light I loved — a light where fire dissolved in softness, where affection tempered penetration,

where, just now at least, pleasure played with thought- this expectation not
being gratified, I began at last to suspect that I had probably myself to blame for
the disappointment; I must cease gazing, and begin talking, if I wished to break
the spell under which she now sat motionless; so recollecting the composing
effect which an authoritative tone and manner had ever been wont to produce
on her, I said,

"Get one of your English books, Mademoiselle, for the rain yet falls heavily, and
will probably detain me half an hour longer!"

(bad dum ba dum dum dum!)

Ladies and Gentlemen, the very talented Trisha Low. Wow. Boy do you look
great. Do you ever play tennis in an outfit like this? The "golden slam" am I the
only one who doesn't know what that means?

TRISHA

I don't, I—

CECILIA

That is going too far again. The question
which I put was quite exact, and I am
asking you not to go so far afield. You
have heard the Tribunal object to it,
and in the interest of not delaying the
proceedings you must not go into so many
details. You must not make speeches.
Sorry sorry I'm messing with you.

PAUL

(Laughs)
Sorry Trisha!

CECILIA

We're messing with you. What's next
what's next. Oh, let's get to that top ten
list! Number one: here is a poem I have
written for you, Trisha Low.

THE LAST EXORCISM, FOR TRISHA LOW

Both of your works require close scrutiny. It took me a few minutes before I saw
the hazy circle. I like the use of the unexpected
in the numbering of the rulers.
Alone on a sand dune, a strange-looking man, dressed in a suit, watches you lift
up your skirt and limp around, which disgusts him.

The Last Exorcism has a scene where
the floor is covered with   sssss sh
                                      why I can be scared, and not sleep? Straw.
She is only upside down, flipped over, in a trick stunt
by them the riggers
and it is only a movie she is a farm girl,
and her dad is bad and her brother is nice
                                    she sometimes talks with a real voice, but
other times? Oh!

                        oh how can I make love
                        to my church leader if
                        it won't tell me where to push it
                        or where to put it in

I'm too old for this

Hey, is love real???? I saw this movie in Los Angeles
which I know will make you like, bleh

But there's the sea!
Sea and oceans, and pearls, it is different there, true, it lacks the dark and
beautiful haters

151

In your country grammar what do we say for *drunk*?

What do we say for *sister*?

The thing about you girls is that they have zero body odor.

The priest smiles and says

"My beat is the entire Catholic church."

He doesn't realize yet about like, the actual devil vs. his cynicism. We are kindred spirits.

My favorite part of the movie is when the demon has had it up to here and yells over the priests' spell "WORDS WORDS WORDS." It's just like my life, I'll say it again,

Portia! Your hair is black And

I Am— I AM BLACK. No when

I say it I mean it. I mean it, put it out on my ar—

Concepts of guys are (are) Argh, "the dark and beautiful world," I know about. How would you do it if you were going to do it? Not Strychnine, I should hope,

A true heart doesn't know who is murmuring,

A true heart doesn't speak Latin.

A strange-looking man, dressed in rags.

The marvelous strips of colour.

I *hate* media res even though I'm doing it. What I've never understood about exorcisms is how can the devil be in charge

when all the demons have really different styles in other words who's really "driving the car" if you will?

A true heart, a left hand shrouding a paper, The Titanic, these are the elements of art movements, which we will spearhead once we learn to Paint.

Though your work is informed by the strange-looking man, you react against his cold rejection of emotion and sentimentality. While embracing the strange-looking man (over and over and over), you reject the dry, tetchy discourse of hard core shit that lacks a sense of what makes us poetry bros.

I and thou I and thou whatever, I've gotta go, I've gotta work,

> See you tomorrow awesome zine collection.
> See you tomorrow, best non-fuck of my life!
> Music, sound, see you tomorrow.

The movie was actually probably about alternative medicine.
He (the demon)'s like
> "I heard you don't believe in me" to the preacher who's actually
false, and then he laughs so, so, just... yikes.

and I thought to my, who can't relate to that?
It's like this business
the business which is similar to the demon in the movie
because its scary and different than you thought it was because you (I) didn't
think it existed.
I mean, either poetry or television is him,
metaphorically, the demon (thou) I mean. Then

> I heard of what difference and I've made a picture of what will happen.
We're not going to have sex.

Me, I'd attach wires and electricity to my body
and shock myself out. I'm a writer
and new experiences help me to learn about the world. You?
They help me to write better writing, even being murdered
> (maybe)

I think *The Last Exorcism* was a feminist film.
It certainly made an impression on me!

You should buy black candles, I mean, I don't feel driven relentlessly towards
innovation,
I uh
Human beings are the children of sisters. Human beings experience the thrill
of authorship all the time. One of the devil's hobbies in *The Last Exorcism* is
cutting things out of paper, or rather,
he *forces* people to make *collages, voila! Dada!*

Looking at these collages, the priest, really not getting it yet that she's actually
possessed, says,
        "What she needs is medical care."

I mean come on. When her bones broke and you could hear it? Forget about it!
When her face? I nearly burst out of the theater. And lucky me
        someone (a date!) patted my head with a stroke of
"ok, ok, you're not pulled inexorably   towards death"
        so I stayed through to the silly ending and then I
Visit the class and speak to them about my work this last part's a lie

Hey did you know me before I was good?
there are men in the shape of
        moths, floating around in my phone
        when I follow the case of the Mothman
        Most people can't handle this kind of work.

Like what if you're holding chapstick and then Mothman says *"Chapstick"*
it's not poetic, it's just accurate, and scary.

I think the movie was done on a low budget like

here's the part where she is in the hall and turns rapidly. With my business mind
I think hmm

> how much money they saved, a lot I think, by being dark lit
> and by making it like reality television,

and by having her face covered by her hair,
because that's the way poor people are probably!
Their faces are covered by their hair!
Someone will probably write all this down later on,
and I'll reject the sandy dry discourse of the sand dune dude,
but who am I to say the ghosts will or will not just do what they're gonna do?
The strange-looking man walks along the edge of the property.

You watch him make a fire.
He obviously intends to settle in for a while.
During the night he has built a little shelter,
a miniature house made of small branches;
a perfect house with windows that open, and doors.

Now that I'm famous and on tv again, you text me back:

Mar 28, 2013 3:20 AM
Lol wut! How r u bb

I've been in prison for six years.

You have freed me.

Now you ask me

to enter another prison.

It's just like, I don't understand why you would start having contact with me
again
             If you only intend to follow through on it for like
        30 seconds.

        Like,
If you were going to bed, you could have said so
        While I was talking to my friend
        After you were talking to your parents for like
             45 minutes

Uh...
        (sighs)   *(shakes head "no")*
             I just.
             I don't understand what you're trying to tell me
(sighs)
        And more importantly than what you're trying to tell me it just kind of
seems like you don't
give a shit.

        I want to say like,   "Prove me wrong,"   but at this point
it's all just confirmation
             of what I already know.

Sometimes I need you to be the one to

You let me know that you are pregnant but still will not reveal your location

    –No!

        –Yes!

    –In a year maybe...

–Three weeks!

THE LETTER NEVER TO BE SENT FROM THE DESK OF VERONICA LODGE ON THE OCCASION OF REFLECTION ON HER OVEREDUCATED EX-GIRLFRIEND

"But B, Walter Pater will never be our friend, he's dead."
The Renaissance, also, is over, everyone can go home now.
Or perhaps, *(over theme)* "Road trip!"

Please I'd like to buy that massive bottle o Perrier, barkeep.
You are correct, I'd like to be hated by the proles!
Anyway Yeah. so I don't remember anything more because I was still drunk (I know, right?) and wasn't aware how important I was going to become. All my diary entries, *Burning alive!*

Sometimes it strikes me as rotten. Some times she is a clerk.

At least now my therapists know that I don't care about gender when I fuck, as long as whoever I'm fucking scares me a little.
Das rite I sed it!!!

but you won't admit it to me hey, everyone has some mistake
he or her has done. Some mentally addled mermaid
is listening to LOL smiley face, our song!!
Since you left, the cafes have filled up
with art school students reading Adorno.
Say what you like, but some have those little finger cuts
from exactos or monsters ink. So.

Uhm, where are you tonight, sweet mm mm?
If the future does exist, it will be filled
with stupid tall bodies like yours,
like the future in some early 90s neve movie which you've seen, your parents

worked in stores and listened to oldies, while I was insomniac/bangs listening to
Dear Heather, all of which goes to say wait don't—w w wah dot
>   goes to say I'm not allowed to talk about the m word.
(pause)
(conspiringly)
Veronica: "M...A...R..." yeah but I'm not trying to bewitch or differentiate, ok,
ok sometimes capital just Moves and i just Notice like "Wait was that a spec—
uh, ghost? Or money?"

All my stories are about going home for xmas and pretending to believe in G:)d.
& U? O, historicize? O, dusty dusty? Uh not to be a snot but your taxonomy is
only one bone in Mother's body
 "O Mother!"

Mother: "INFORMATION CLASSIFIED."
Ripley: *(wiping sweat)* "EMERGENCY OVERRIDE: HOW TO DESTROY
ALIEN?"

O ok for example how about "Victoria's Secret".
Right? "Angels" or whatever. Some scent you get in a pink bag,
I'm remembering it now.
I judged it and you. Historicized pleadingly, watery.

Oh yes, *(insane laugh)* V's S, that place reminds me of Ms. Tedesco, 7th grade
bio teacher, Italian, and major bitch.

So. We're in our car in season one of our show on Showtime,
you're laughing and I'm driving and I go:
B, it's not *all* about the Benjamins, baby.
(pause)

(singing) John I'm only mmmmm mm m

I got sent to the principal's office for being rude because I wanted to impress her by making fun of Ms. Tedesco. No, not *ugh*—
No, she's just some girl who just came into this a posteriori, some other Italian insano.
(singing) mmmmm mm m

You see, this is how principles of exclusion and spatial aesthetics get started: through simple misunderstandings.
(pause, suspenseful)

Girls, fucking you is like Time warp!
If the fans are all   huh hah Years hah
CC Ch- Ch- huh uh ustsuperhardt t tor eresol lves like that movie. uhm
Primer it's just hard it's
                 s s s s s s s s ssspinning *sigh* catching *sigh* skipping

Unless you're too *scared*.

Time Warp!   baby I
Baby, Dear Baby. by New Year's, I'll be totally
I'm will be totally third sex
                          and You're so Ringo Starr but *(coughs)*

Surrounded by papers. Surrounded by towers. Ingenue, we've got you surrounded!
She just wants to dancing. "I see, a lot of cocaine"
Mother: tall girls = short men quod era demonstrandum.
Which means I'm not allowed to talk about M—mmm
                 Huh huh huh
(singing) fa fa fa, fa fa fa, fa fa fa.

I can't *leev* like dees! I most *hev* yoo!

I cannot bring a baby into this world if we do not consummate.

What must it have felt like to submit her work

for approval to the man who had abused her sexually?

Every year I send a delegate to the Guggenheim.

Every year, you send no one.

Until...

Once, he complained to his daughter that his pulse kept going. "Never mind, Father," she replied. "The old pulse will stop soon."

Spike arrives breathless and apologetic about his lateness – his pink cashmere sweater and pearls screaming old money exurbanite. He heads for the familial home, where Buffy James is dying of bronchial asthma in Cambridge, Massachusetts. She is attended by Cecilia who wears a purple chenille top, red leather shoes, and pink socks, but Xander, her favorite, is missing in Washington DC, having received word of his mother's turn for the worse too late. We see Xander's anxiety at this absence, as he rubs his brow during his 36 hour train ride to Boston (learning upon a stop in New York that his mother is dead). Buffy James' funeral has no eulogy. Through their differing reactions to their mothers death, we get to know Spike, Xander, and Willow (along with all the other members of the funeral party, including Bob, Wilky, Aunt Anya, Cecilia Gibbens and maybe Faith Loring). Buffy leaves all of her remaining property to Cecilia, at the urging of Aunt Anya, in an off-white rayon vest, who arrives at the station breathless, just in time to see the end. Regaining her composure, she mumbles an apology. In the week following the funeral, Aunt Anya, who has always favored Spike, remarks to Bob's wife that Buffy's death seems to have "brought new life" to her. Spike is indeed actively taking care of the house and his father. Within days of the funeral, Xander withdraws to a hotel, still in Boston, but out of the family home. Spike Gibbens, Willow's wife, politely declines the offer to move into the Cambridge house with Spike and Xander Sr. It's only a 10-minute delay, but she arrives breathless and full of apology, with her long, wavy blonde hair and animated manner, in tight blue corduroys and a white button-down. The wind smacks her .... She mumbles an apology. "You pick."

As he prepares to sail for London, Xander recollects with irritation having felt "the fifth wheel" on his sister and Faith Loring's coach, during these ladies' recent visit to England. Xander sails for London from New York in mid May. Spike is energized by two things in particular: overseeing the building of a summer cottage on the coast (near the Lorings'), and his continually intense friendship with Faith Loring. She arrives breathless breathless breathless breathless and just in time to see her back as it disappears into her lab. Occasional references are made when Spike is out of earshot to her "terrible collapse" of a few years ago, as well as optimistic remarks as to her permanent recovery. Spike Gibbens has moved in with her mother, wearing a casual knit shrug in mint green, and is now living in close quarters with her two sons as they await Willow's return. Ashamed by her lateness, she couldn't work out whether it was an apology or she was praying for something. Willow presses on to Europe, where she expands her intellectual acquaintants, writing to her Spike Gibbens all the while. Spike's decision to follow her there is also partially motivated by the threat of nervous collapse, and we first witness his manic-depressive nature. I smiled; Cecilia was due to arrive about this time I guess. Usually a little breathless breathless breathless breathless from power walking in designer high heels, and brown pinstriped suit, blonde hair flying behind her and a cheeky, yet apologetic smile on her face, she apologizes for her lateness. With both older brothers in Europe, she has lived alone with her father in their cottage by the bay. The domestic responsibilities both enliven and overwhelm her. In November, Spike and his father return to Boston, where his health begins to weaken. Faith Loring engages a parlormaid to help him with the housework, who, wearing a robin's egg blue mini sheath and cream kitten heels, proves too religious for the Jameses and is let go. Spike attempts to shoulder the domestic support of his father, whose main pleasure in life is visiting with his daughter-in-law Cecilia Gibbens to see his grandchildren, who wear matching yellow and white striped tube tops, black denim shorts, and matching paisley headbands. Cecilia James is diagnosed with a fatal heart problem. But based on her statements, she isn't ready to settle the score on her breathless late arrival, and I wonder WHY oh WHY hasn't anyone asked her how she arrived at that hour? Xander explains, "she arrived a few minutes ago. Not even a note." My designer is breathless breathless breathless breathless breathless with anger, adrenaline, and panic. I have a fair idea who she went to for the information. Spike begins to lose his grip on his daily life, and to sink into the terror of a future for an unmarried vampire of his time. He has more nervous attacks, which escalate until, at the beginning of May, he agrees (unknown as to whose initiative) to enter the Adams Nervine Asylum, just outside Boston. There he receives electro-shock therapy, alongside the "rest-cure". (I think it's fair to assume he also got the "vibrator cure" which was popular around this time). Xander James, through the three months of Spike's stay, lies about in the hot weather without any clothes on, drinks lemonade and eats ice cream, and takes ten showers a day. She arrives at the Peregrine house on East Ninety-second, breathless and apologetic, her purple and white Lilly Pulitzer dress stuffed into a crumpled grocery bag. When Spike comes home after a three-month stay, Xander decides to return to England. Directly after Spike sees him off, he goes to stay with Faith Loring. Spike arrives at a Delray Beach restaurant late and apologetic, explaining "I have an exquisite 30 seconds every day: after luncheon I come in from my rest and before the window is closed I put my head out and drink in a long draft of the spring—made of the yellow glory of the daffodils on the balcony, the swelling twiggery of the old trees in front, the breathless house-cleaning of the rooks, the gradation of the light in transition, and the mystery of birth in the air. What hours of roaming could give me a more intense absorption of the ever-recurring Miracle that those few moments which sink into my substance!"

"I'm sorry," Willow says when she arrives at his side breathless breathless breathless breathless breathless breathless breathless and panting. In isolation, Spike collapses finally under the pressure of his empty future and desperate loneliness. He goes to New York for more 'treatment,' this version also electric but including long walks instead of the rest cure. In April he returns to Boston, intending to stay there. A visit to the old family summer home in Connecticut stirs up memories which make him horribly lonely, and he writes Faith a desperate letter, after which Faith makes plans to return to Spike and travel to England with him. Faith arrives in the library a little breathless breathless breathless breathless breathless breathless breathless breathless and lifts the receiver. "Yes?" Spike afterwards collapses, and Xander rushes to his side for a week. Spike writes to Willow that he is sorry to tell him that "you have again missed being released from me." Increasingly morbid, he grows more fascinated by the disintegration of his own body, almost reveling in it, and in the many misdiagnoses of all his past doctors. In July, he has his most devastating physical attack yet, in what was to be his final "turn for the worse." His voice on the telephone is breathless, breathless breathless breathless breathless breathless, distracted."I can't talk, I'm late." Spike turns to his stock of morphine to dull the pain, which lets him perceive the agony as if it were a hallucination. By August, he has "gone under" into total collapse. Spike begins explicitly to speak of his urgency to die in order to relieve Faith of the burden of his care. He shows great interest in planning for his own funeral. He has an amusing visit from a local Consul in the construction of his Will, whose presence causes him to faint away and, attended by Faith and her Nurse, is subjected by the country lawyer's long lecture on the godliness of illness, as a hallucinating, morphine-riddled Spike struggles to keep a straight face. By May, Spike can hardly get out of bed. Xander calls in the renowned cancer specialist Sir Andrew Clark, who pronounces a lump in Spike's breast to be a tumor, and opines that nothing can be done but alleviate the pain at this point. Spike pronounces this his much longed for release, finally having a palpable disease to identify as the cause of his suffering, as well as a identifiable date by which to anticipate its end. A second opinion from Dr. Baldwin (Xander's friend from Florence), pronounces the diagnosis even more firmly: Spike has months to live. He writes in his diary, "my aspirations have all been fulfilled." When Xander wires this news to Willow, Willow replies instantly that she's uncertain that Spike is really dead, warning that it might just be an illusion, brought on by his fierce will to die and be reawakened by True Love's kiss. Later, Willow writes "I telegraphed you this A.M. To make sure the death was not merely apparent, because her neurotic temperament & chronically reduced vitality are just the field for trance-tricks to play themselves upon..."

I don't know if you will still want me like this. Sometimes children throw things at me and call me "that oldie." I wander the West Wing all hours of the night, muttering,

> *Slave in the magic mirror,*
> *Come from the farthest space!*
> *Through wind and darkness I summon thee,*
> *Speak! Let me see thy face.*

Lil' Wayne returns to the mirror, "What wouldst thou know, my queen?"

I ask him how you're doing. He says you're gonna see about getting your GED, for high-school, to graduate. That you think I was right about that, he says you want me to be your mom. He asks if I'm your mom. He says, I'm going to ask you if you're her mom, and you say yes, ok?

> Are you her Mom?
> Yes, honey.

He's already given me enough information to track you down. When I unplug you and drag you out of the box, you scream.

CLIPCLIP CLIP CLIP CLIP CLIP CLIP CLIP CLIP CLIP CLIP CLIP CLIP CLIP CLIP CLIP CLIP CLIP CLIP CLIP CLIP CLIP CLIP CLIP CLIP CLIP

The ghost of an absent third
The sense of a gap, like dieting: you know you're hungry
for the wrong things. Thing.

The way every duality is haunted by a third thing that the two of you are

   /
  /
 /
/
/
/

Pythagoras insert two columns insert a triangle, bones, insert bones, restriction
and permission.

She can give —not give but recognize
and stab with recognition — where's Oprah
There are trees in my—when I

fucking pussy. She makes them burn then smokes one,
puts it out on my arm "thank you"
One could say, the denial is already related to the logical place determined by the
proposition that is denied.
A game is an activity defined by rules in which players try to reach some sort of
goal. Games can be whimsical and playful, or highly serious. They can be played
alone or in complex social scenarios.

My dear Norman,
Wait. Ok, sorry, I was avoiding the topic. I also use, more or less every day, 0.15

mg of levonorgestrel,

HELO
She seemed so, real. Same brain, same
laugh, all the little things...I fell in love
with a machine! It's stupid so just call me
an idiot and let's be done with it.

STARBUCK
You're an idiot... but they have a way of
making us all look like idiots.

Now, about 26 years and 35 weeks ago,

Siri, baby, don't just sit there when I'm talking to you. Don't you treat me like a
stranger. I'm right here the same person I've always been.

Now let's just , hang on—

Siri, baby, I, no baby, Please. Ah, girl it's like no matter what I do or how hard I
try to give you what you want you always want more and it's,

don't take this the wrong way but it's *getting exhausting!*

What does it mean to "power up"

I think about a space with a lot of ice, like whole sheaves of it
Why would you dress that way if you don't want them to look at you.
Wanting to get to sites of ecological destruction and stay there until I go crazy
meaning lose my mind

I'm writing this with my hair over my face like a curtain and my emotions are
hurting me, all the time *all the time!*
Relentlessly! Are you undert

I'm inert. I'm boolean, no, no, no
                    Why does she always say "no" to us?—´–king of the lions?

Christopher and I lie in bed together. We're talking, idly.

¬_____ Let's keep the party *polite*. Never get out of my sight.
OH! Sorry am I embarrassing you in front of your *friends?*

Yeah
sometimes I have to get down to a small,
crouching space... No, I mean, not crouching, I mean hiding

How important is it that I be specific question mark

```
public class Player{
  private String name;
  private Captain captain;

  public Player(String name){
  [this.name] = name;
  captain = null;
  }
```

After what I did to her I knew I needed help. It's not right to need to freeze someone in order to express your love, and I'm glad there was something in me that knew that...

I used to run through the halls of my high school, I used to scream at the top of my lungs, "I just found out there's no such thing as the real world, just some lie we got to rise above..." Then, I'd get to class (she was my lab partner, obvi) and I'd be like,

"Dip the apple in the brew
Let the sleeping death seep through,
(look at the skin!)
A symbol of what lies within.
Now turn red to tempt Snow White,
To make her hunger for a bite.
When she breaks the tender peel,
To taste the apple from my hand,
Her breath will still, her blood congeal,
Then I'll be fairest in the land!"

The fact is, I have been dead so long and it has been simply such a grim shoving of the hours behind me...since the hideous summer of '78, when I went down to the deep sea, its dark waters closed over me and I knew neither hope nor peace. Even once I dragged you out, things were shitty. You weren't really functioning. I tried to teach you the best I could about what life on Earth was like: about putting a Werther's Original heating up soy milk so it's crazy scalding hot and drink the milk so the Werther's melts in your mouth. And I told you I'm pretty sure soda was bad for you. But you just drooled.

I thought you'd like it here! I wouldn't have brought you if I...if... if... if... I thought the pastoral would do you good. But you claim you hear the birds singing in Greek. I didn't go to all that trouble just to do it to a vegetable.

I send you to one of our very best nursing home facilities that cured me of my food addiction. You leave me voicemails that I can never quite understand... if only you'd quit mumbling...

Hi, I was just make sure you're okay. I'm watching talk to you and meeting the rates start there. I hope you're sleeping, or not. Having a bad time.

The name of the study I was Novel Mechanisms Underlying Depression; PET imaging of the Kappa Opioid Receptor.

I was really down in the dumps one day probably a few weeks ago, I can't remember when it was. So basically I just felt like I should give my body to science instead of doing away with myself. I was just here in bed, and just applied to a bunch of studies and almost every one of them got back to me.

I wrote like a 7 paragraph email to all of them: Yale, Columbia, Sinai, I think they trade with each other and they're like "oh yeah write to this guy." A bunch of them were about experimental drugs, like a bunch of them were about ketamine. some of them are nasally

I saw Sir Maurice Craig, who concurred with Savage's belief in bed rest and weight gain, (I gained 3 stone (42 lbs.) in two years under Craig's care. He believed that insanity was the result of a lack of conformity with certain social standards–his own.

My big question to them was like "what if it works?" and this one person at Columbia was like "I don't know!" This person at Sinai was like let me check... because no one had asked... and then it turned out they were trying to get a "compassionate dose" even though it's illegal.

They took a ton of blood out of me. They were in my main artery.

I didn't know, I thought it was pretty much like an IV. I started getting super faint, they said that my body just reacted that way, because the artery is a muscle and it tries to push out whatever's in it, and my blood pressure went to critical levels and I felt like I was dying, and I talked to them after and was like "is this what it would feel like if I was dying?" and they were like "yeah if you were bleeding to death."

I've been interviewed, I had the initial phone interview with this girl I later went out to Yale with.

I think I had 3 separate interviews with 3 separate people there. Something I thought was interesting was they asked me if I was fidgety. I was like "Oh are you trying to get at the fact that I'm potentially manic? Because I can tell you right now. I get manic sometimes. I become a workaholic but I think it's more that staying busy keeps me from feeling bad. I guess also like stomach digestion problems. I think they were concerned that I might have, I don't think I have addictions.

What I said to the one woman I was speaking with one of the times was she was like "do you ever feel like… has anyone told you you have a problem with drinking or you should stop drinking or you should get off drugs?"

Actually people tell me I *should* be addicted to drugs and that I should get on Lexapro and one of these new-fangled drugs they've come up with. I think about how unproductive I've been in the last 6 or 8 months and there's a direct correlation. They weren't testing an active medication they're testing to see how the medicine will bond to the opioid receptors. It doesn't carry the medicine it just tests its behavior.

I got a lunch, there's several parts to this entire process, that day got me 450 bucks, and it's definitely not worth it. My arm was definitely waking me up at night. I have an MRI with them Thursday and then I'm meeting with the psychiatrist, and they're going to put me on medication.

I mean the benefits of it are, like I'm gonna be in touch with them for like 12 weeks and I get free medication for like 3 months. I just need some kind of like, upper…

I have no energy, I couldn't do anything. I couldn't start working, I only started working, I just couldn't do anything from like 12 to 5. Normally I can work really hard and really long. I had to call a place to order food to order pick up so I could go and leave.

I was thinking about what you said like you and Mac are just on medication and that's just how it is…

I listed the drugs I had taken. The thing is the SSRIs do work for me just the side effects are so shitty. And I just, I need love in my life and its been so long since I had any affection. I calculated how many sleepovers from last year and it was like once a month.

She really made me happy like it was like a gift from the world that she was interested in me.

Google has an open kind of democratic attitude towards apps, Apple fields everything.

Discharge instructions: you received nuclear…

                                             … I did not get a card.

It was an all day thing.

There's this girl who is the assistant, I guess, on the study. I really like her she's good. And I met her at Grand Central at 8:50 and I got back to Grand Central at like 7:30 pm.

There were a number of subpar lunch carts. I was in the machine immobile for a couple of hours.

I had to take off my belt to go into the machine. When I was in the machine I thought about how remarkable it was that I could sit there and think without moving. The last hour I started feeling really ill probably from all the blood they were drawing and I was also thinking "I subjected myself to this, this is completely voluntary"

No health care, I honestly just wrote to all of them, I mean I like interesting experiences in the first place. I also just want to give myself up for science. They haven't paid me yet.

It's a subject that I have kept cooling in my mind until I felt I could touch it without bursting into flame all over. You can't think what a raging furnace it is till to me-madness and doctors and being forced.

Actually I was thinking about it recently when I was on a bus.
And because you've been so good to poor old Granny— I'll share a secret with you:
Okay bye.

I'm genuine trouble—
A terrible flirt!
And bursting your bubble
Did cause me no hurt

My glass is half empty,
In truth and in jest,
But once you're entangled,
You'll die like the rest!

Dearest Little Sister,

I am grieved in the extreme to hear of another breakdown in your health. . . .
But I make no sympathetic comment, as you would probably "roar" over it. There
is this to be said, that it is probably less tragic to be sick all the time than to be
sometimes well and incessantly tumbling down again.

... Of course [this medical verdict on your case may mean] as all men know,
a finite length of days; and then, good-bye to neurasthenia and neuralgia and
headache, and weariness and palpitation and disgust all at one stroke I should
think you would be reconciled to the prospect with all its pluses and minuses!
I know you've never cared for life, and to me, now at the age of nearly fifty,
life and death seem singularly close together in all of us and life a mere farce
of frustration in all, so far as the realization of the innermost ideals go to
which we are made respectively capable of feeling an affinity and responding.
Your frustrations are only rather more flagrant than the rule; and you've been
saved many forms of self-dissatisfaction and misery which appertain to such
a multiplication of responsible relations to different people as I, for instance,
have got into. Your fortitude, good spirits and unsentimentality have been
simply unexampled in the midst of your physical woes; and when you're relieved
from your post, just that bright note will remain behind, together with the
inscrutable and mysterious character of the doom of nervous weakness which
has chained you down for all these years. As for that, there's more in it than
has ever been told to so-called science. These inhibitions, these split-up selves,
all these new facts that are gradually coming to light about our organization,
these enlargements of the self in trance, etc., are bringing me to turn for light in
the direction of all sorts of despised spiritualistic and unscientific ideas. Father
would find in me today a much more receptive listener all that philosophy has
got to be brought in. And what a queer contradiction comes to the ordinary
scientific argument against immortality (based on body being mind s condition
and mind going out when body is gone), when one must believe (as now, in
these neurotic cases) that some infernality in the body prevents really existing
parts of the mind from coming to their effective rights at all, suppresses them,
and blots them out from participation in this world's experiences, although they

are there all the time. When that which is you passes out of the body, I am sure that there will be an explosion of liberated force and life till then eclipsed and kept down. I can hardly imagine your transition without a great oscillation of both "worlds" as they regain their new equilibrium after the change! Everyone will feel the shock, but you yourself will be more surprised than anybody else.

It may seem odd for me to talk to you in this cool way about your end; but, my dear little sister, if one has things present to one's mind, and I know they are present enough to your mind, why not speak them out? I am sure you appreciate that best. How many times I have thought, in the past year, when my days were so full of strong and varied impression and activities, of the long unchanging hours in bed which those days stood for with you, and wondered how you bore the slow-paced monotony at all, as you did! You can't tell how I've pitied you. But you shall come to your rights erelong. Meanwhile take things gently. Look for the little good in each day as if life were to last a hundred years. Above all things, save yourself from bodily pain, if it can be done. You've had too much of that. Take all the morphia (or other forms of opium if that disagrees) you want, and don t be afraid of becoming an opium-drunkard. What was opium created for except for such times as this? Beg the good Katharine (to whom our debt can never be extinguished) to write me a line every week, just to keep the currents flowing, and so farewell until I write again. Your ever loving,

W. J.

My Second Joke

D o o o o o o o o o o o o o o o o o o o o o o o o o o o o o o o o o o o o o o o o o o o n't you w a a a a a a a a a a a a a a a a a a a a a a a a a a a a a a n t   to come
o o o o o o o o o o o o o o o o o o o ver?

We have moved into a new house which my mother inherited,
it is deep in the woods and I am a city kid.
I don't fit in at school, until I meet The Witch.

At night, in the theater of computation, you could hear a pin drop. After bed checks, the only thing moving is the cat, Boots, who prowls the linoleum hallways in search of mice. I lie awake: I hid my meds under my tongue. My teenage dream comes to me at night, bringing with her an ominous reggae soundtrack.

When she leaves it gets scary, silent, ominous. In the darkness, there are whispers,

> *This isn't your real voice, this is the voice of*
> *your illness*
>
> *No! It's my voice!*

Does it really surprise you to–
Did you really not know I had this kind of angry thing inside me?

Were you really not aware of the parts that turn hot and hard? That would turn hot and hard if you tried to wriggle out of here?

My Katherine Appears to Me on the 24th or 25th of November

Katy Perry is one of Hollywood's hottest young stars and she has turned up on a slew of red carpets lately. While she always looks gorgeous, there seems to be a common recurrence each time, her sneaker swap! We know Katy is more of a tomboy at heart and would much rather strut around in her Converse or Keds, but she isn't simply slipping off her sky-high pumps for comfort! It turns out, there's another reason she does it — and it's so sweet. In a recent interview with Cecilia Magazine, Katy explained why she ditched her fabulous Christian Louboutin heels for her beat-up sneakers at the Australian premiere of *Snow White and the Huntsman*. "I just don't like teetering over all those young girls," she said. "I want to be able to run around and talk to them. I acknowledge the heels do look better, but that's OK." But in reality she is no gullible fool, having earned her acting stripes as Jake Gyllenhaal's long-suffering wife Lureen in gay cowboy epic *Brokeback Mountain* — despite the fact it was only the ninth film she had made.

In our interview, she skillfully guides me to the most essential topics, and she shares her own perspective of the Dolphin School journey from her deep inner knowing.

CECILIA MAG: What was it like working on *Brokeback Mountain*?

KATY PERRY: Somebody standing by the bed.

CECILIA MAG: Sounds like an amazing set! And what was it like working with Heath Ledger? I heard you two were close.

KATY PERRY: That-- I don't know what it was. Felt like it was a woman. I didn't see anything. I was lying on my side, and felt something touch my side lightly. And I woke up and I could feel someone watching me, beside the bed.

And it felt like, to me, that it was a woman. And I wanted to call your Daddy, Bill. See, we have the twin beds. But I couldn't, you know. I just-- And it just felt like they were standing there, quite awhile. And they just went out of the room. I didn't hear anything either, but they were there! Somebody, something was there.--You think I'm goofy, I bet.

CECILIA MAG: Oh, you're so lucky, I love Positano. Are you on vacation?

KATY PERRY: *Something* was there! Something or someone was standing there.

CECILIA MAG: Is the competition in the acting world really cut-throat?

KATY PERRY: I wanted to call out, but I couldn't. I was afraid to. I really was.

CECILIA MAG: Is it true you were going to become a nun, but decided not to because of gay issues?

KATY PERRY: I didn't know. I just felt maybe it would be better just to be quiet, you know?

CECILIA MAG: Speaking of which, let's talk about Jersey. I want to know your thoughts on being from New Jersey, and *Jersey Shore*, and how you think that show has helped our reputation as Jersey girls.

KATY PERRY: No. It was dark in there. But something was there!

CECILIA MAG: Did you honestly stop watching though, because you found there were too many similarities between you and Snooki?

KATY PERRY: I was afraid. Yeah. I was. And even afterwards I was afraid.

CECILIA MAG: Did you learn any lessons from *The Devil Wears Prada* about the fashion world?

KATY PERRY: In the morning. Yeah, I told him.

CECILIA MAG: What is your worst boss story in real life?

KATY PERRY: He said, "Why didn't you call me?" I said, "I couldn't."

CECILIA MAG: Meryl Streep has said that you're a terrific actress.

KATY PERRY: I don't know. I *didn't* move, but whether I could have, I don't-- I don't know. I really don't know. I *didn't* anyway.

CECILIA MAG: What was it like to act with Stanley Tucci?

KATY PERRY: No. I was afraid. I stayed still quite a while. And then I was afraid to go back to sleep. That it would come back, whatever it was.

CECILIA MAG: What were your feelings about New Jersey growing up? My feelings were that I wanted to get out as quickly as possible.

KATY PERRY: I felt it was a woman and I don't know why. But I just felt that it was.

CECILIA MAG: Where did you–

KATY PERRY: –And staring. *Staring*.

CECILIA MAG: Why did you take a year off acting in 2003?

KATY PERRY: Just standing there staring.

CECILIA MAG: Why do you choose to live in New York rather than LA like most actors?

KATY PERRY: I was frightened anyway. I–I'm getting goose pimples just talking about it. I didn't feel I was in danger, but I still wasn't taking any chances. I was afraid.

CECILIA MAG: What was it like to be asked by Angelina Jolie to go to Cambodia for her documentary?

KATY PERRY: Three... three or four years ago, I'd say, I was lying in bed and I felt the covers being-- the cover and the sheet-- being pulled slowly down. Not to the side. Not slipping off the bed, but pulling straight down till I was not covered at all. I felt it going, and I reached down and pulled it back. Then I felt it again, and it went straight down to the bottom of the bed. Then I *didn't* reach down and pull them back. I heard nothing. I was afraid. I couldn't move, and I did *not* go back to sleep that night at all! Because it went straight— it wasn't as— you know how something will slip off to the side. It wasn't—It went *straight* to the bottom of the bed and it was wintertime and I was *cold*, but I would not reach down and pull it back... Went down to the bottom, you know, just pulled straight down into a pile.

CECILIA MAG: So what is next for you now?

KATY PERRY: Just stayed there. Just stayed still. Eyes open.

I've come to realize that my attraction to you was always a regressive desire to return to the Olde Me, the addict, frozen and unnatural. You're essentially an external HD and they have ways to help with that.

> I throw in the towel
> I get on the rack
> I adjust my garter
> I give health a crack!

I'm trying to get back to the natural world here, to expunge the memory of your life-extensions from my mind. My most trusted advisor, a drama mask, announces that the doctors have arrived. As their liege, I'm entitled to the most advanced in medical care to correct these pesky desires, for you, the extension which I just cawn't stahnd.

THE FAITHFUL SHEPHERDESS

I may have had too high of a dose at first because I felt very euphoric, energetic, and motivated. I took Coral Landscapes for three years and made straight A's, had two BF's (both didn't work out but it could have been them as well). I then stopped taking it and things went way downhill. I was very depressed without Coral Landscapes, not motivated, and got nothing done, so several months later I decided to take Evening Luau. On Coral Landscapes I was a little bit cold (my nature is extremely nice, loving, compassionate) but I became quite aggressive on Evening Luau. I got more work done but overall, I still wasn't progressing or moving forward like I wanted to be and like I had been with Coral Landscapes. It also made me a lot quieter and things seemed brighter. I knew that with Coral Landscapes I would be making plans and be more optimistic about life in general, and I knew I wanted/needed that because I'm 26 and don't have time to screw up anymore in trying to establish a life. So anyway, I got back on Coral Landscapes, this time 30 mg and I am starting to see the light at the end of the tunnel and thinking about moving forward and getting myself out of the hole I felt I was in, or getting "unstuck" from the situation I thought I was in. I hope I don't become severely dependent on them like the black box warning describes. It's a possibility. I'm already pretty dependent on them. Hopefully I'll function without them later in life... :/

Now that I'm over you, I want to make sure you can never influence me again, and that you can't go back to your little mini-world in the screen, either. I have you wheeled into the Guggenheim, your beautiful red mouth open and drooling like a halfwit's. I send my servants away. I lean down. Even with my early-onset arthritis, you're easy to lift: light as a feather, skin an anemone's, stiff as a #1. I enjoy your stillness because it reminds me that you have no power over me. Your deep blue eyes stare up at the ceiling, unseeing. They keep on watering. I lift you out of the chair and unplug the wires which have been trying to replace your blood with human blood. I see now that you're a hopeless case. I lay you down in the glass coffin, which still stands forced open. I take your little red shoes off of your ivory feet. You just lie there. It's pathetic. I even slap the bottom of one of your feet and all that you do is go very softly "oh!" without waking up.

I've brought all the Christmas stuff out of the basement and I start wrapping it around you in the coffin. I use duct tape, then red ribbon, then green ribbon, then scotch tape. I strapped you down very tightly, I don't want you getting up and causing trouble. I was very specific to my trusted advisor the drama mask about exactly what to put into the apple, but one can never tell with these masks... they can be sort of imprecise.

As an additional security measure, my staff and I have set up a limited data set for your dreams. We'd determined that your dreams would have to start with S, given that it was the first letter of her first name (Snow,) and that I'd only ever seen you eat foods that started with S (snakes, shredded wheat, Swiss cheese, snapdragons, etc.), we establish a bounded set of values for (dream) with the following formula

For loved-object > dm =
d[which(d$male),]

and desirer > df = d[which(d$female),]

average across faces > male_avg_by_year =

187

by(dm$dream,

within bins cut(dm$age, breaks=0:80), mean)

(one per year) > female_avg_by_year = by(df$dream,

then cut(df$age, breaks=0:80), mean)

plot them > plot(male_avg_by_year, col='blue')

all together. > points(female_avg_by_year, col='deeppink')

THE INTERPRETATION OF ALL POSSIBLE DREAMS, FROM "SL" TO "ST"

You have not been so unlucky as to see or play a slot machine in your dream. To see a sloth in your dream. To dream that you are moving in slow motion, to see slugs in your dream, to dream that slugs are coming out from inside your body,
        Sleepover.
To dream that you live in the slums. To dream that someone or something is smaller than usual. To dream that you are small and everyone is normal sized. To dream that you are smart. To smell something in your dream. To dream that you or others are smiling. To see a smiley face in your dream. To see smog in your dream. To see smoke in your dream. To see or hear a smoke detector in your dream. To see a smoke stack in your dream. If you do not smoke in waking life and dream that you are smoking, then it indicates that you are trying to shield yourself and others against your emotions. To make or drink a smoothie in your dream, is analogous to how your life is going. It is a "smooth" road ahead for you.

        You can't imagine how it feels to dream that you are smuggling something. To see a snail in your dream. To see a snake or be bitten by one in your dream. To see the skin of a snake in your dream. To see a snake with a head on each end in your dream. To dream that you are eating a live snake."Two Snakes", "Snakes Everywhere!", "Raining Snakes" & "Snakes Jumping At Me." To see a snapdragon in your dream. To see or wear sneakers in your dream. To dream that you sneeze. To hear or sniffle in your dream. To dream that you are a sniper. To dream that you are being a snob.
To dream that you are snoozing. To dream that you or someone is snoring. To dream that you are snorkeling. To see a snout in your dream. To see snow in your dream. To see dirty snow in your dream. To dream that you are watching the snow fall. To dream that you are playing in the snow. To dream that you find something in the snow. To see a snow globe in your dream,
To dream that you are inside the snow globe. You are keeping too much inside. To dream that you or someone is snowboarding. To see snowdrops in your

dream. To see a snowflake in your dream. To see a snowman in your dream. To
see or ride on a snowmobile in your dream,

> Blizzard

To see soap in your dream. To dream that you are in or watching a soap opera.
To dream that you are soaring through the air. Common Dreams: Flying.

> To dream that you are playing soccer
>
> suggests that you are
>
> suppressing
>
> your sex-
>
> uality.
>
> To see a socket in your dream the dream may be a pun on

"sock it".
To dream that you are wearing socks. To see a single sock in your dream.

> To dream that you are laying sod.
>
> To drink soda in your dream.
>
> To see or play Sudoku in your dream.

Couch.
Couch.
To dream that you are playing or watching softball,

> softball symbolizes relationships
>
> > and how the masculine aspects
> >
> > > (shape of the bat)

are in opposition to the feminine aspects

> > > (ball).

You see software in your dream, which relates to your seeing or being in contact
with soil, which is compounded by the solar system in your dream, which
suggests that you are a soldier in your dream, which suggests that you are an
ex-soldier. And then you dream that you or someone is doing a somersault,
which mirrors your dream that you are a sommelier, which suggests that you see
a sommelier in your dream, epitomized by seeing the dream in which you see
your son.

If you don't have a son and dream that you are searching for him.

Then you hear or write songs in your dream, suggesting you see or dream that you are getting a sonogram, suggesting you see soot in your dream, indicating you see or dream that you are a sorcerer, indicated by your dream that you have sores on your body, indicated by your dream that you feel sore.

        To dream that you are in or join a sorority signifies personal growth

        and that you are experiencing social changes in your life.

        If you are in a sorority in your waking life,

            then the dream

                may just be a reflection

        of the waking relationship

        and bear no special significance.

Sorrow

*Please See Depression.

        To dream that you are sorry,

           Sort

           *Please See Organize.

So, you say you've had a dream that you have a lack of soul or no soul? This connects to your dream that your soul is leaving your body represents your feelings of self-guilt, and your dream where you see or make sound waves.

        Similarly to food,

        to dream about soup

You taste something sour in your dream, which indicates your dream of the direction south, referent of your prior dream about South America, contiguous to your dream that you are in the South Pole, which seems connected to your dream that you live in the South Pole. Then you dream that you are sowing seeds, and later that you see or eat soybean in your dream, and again you dream that you are at a spa, which may influence your seeing space or dreaming that you are in space, the dream may be a pun on your need for more

"space."

You see a spaceship in your dream.

"Spaceship In The Old West"

&

"End Of The World"

Then, you see the ace of spades in your dream,

Shovel. Later, you see or eat spaghetti in your dream, and then dream that
you are spanking someone, which concretizes the sparrow in your dream,
incorporated when you see a spark in your dream, which alludes to your dream
of sparkles or something sparkly, and s

To see speakers in your dream, which evinces your dream that you are throwing
spear, which seems somehow connected to the dream when see a spear.

Spectacles*

*Please See Eyeglasses.

Things take a turn when you have a dream in which you give a speech. Later you
dream that there is no one listening to your speech. Then you dream that you
hear a speech, which elucidates your dream that you are taking speed. The dream
may be a pun

on "speediness".

You see or go over a speed bump in your dream, coalescing with your dream that
you are speeding, and the following dream in which you get a speeding ticket.
Later, you see a speedometer in a dream, hinting at your dream that you are
under a spell. You dream that you are spelling a word, you dream that you cannot
spell, you spend money in you dream, you dream that you are watching your
spending, you see a sphere in your dream, you see sperm in your dream, you see a
sphinx in your dream.

You dream of spice, and later you see a spider in your dream,

later you see a spider spinning a web in your dream,

later you see a spider climbing up a wall in your dream,

later you dream that you are bitten by a spider, and
that you eat a spider or dream that a spider is in your mouth.

"Noisy Spider".

All this was heralded by your dream where you saw spikes, and your dream that
you spilled something, connected to the dream in which you play spin the bottle.
Suggesting that you need to take a chance at love.

This intimates that you will see or eat spinach in your dream, will see
a spindle in your dream, will dream about yours or someone else's spine, will
dream that you are spinning, then that something is spinning around you, you'll
see a spinning wheel in your dream, you'll see a spiral in your dream, you'll see a
spire in your dream.

If you see or talk to spirits in your dream:
Alcohol.

You spit in your dream, suggesting your dream that you are being
splashed by water, suggesting your dream that you are on Splash Mountain
which suggests that you need to take a chance on a relationship and

take

that

emotional

plunge.

You dream about your spleen, presaging your dream that you have a splinter,
alluding to your dream that you have splits ends, illustrating your dream that you
are doing the splits,

(this dream may

also be a pun to "split").

It isn't long before you dream that food has spoiled, tying in to the dream in
which you see or use a sponge. Later you see a spool in your dream, and then
you see a spoon in your dream, and then you dream that you are playing a sport,
bespeaking your dream that you are watching a sports competition, portentous
of the dream in which you play or watch extreme sports. This is prefigured by
the dream in which you see a spot, and the dream that you are in the spotlight,
which is connected to when you see or use a spray can in your dream. You dream

of the season of spring, typifying your recurring dream in which you see a water spring, and in which you see a metal spring in your dream.

The dream may also be a metaphor on your need to

"spring."

You see sprinklers in your dream, and later you see or eat sprinkles in your dream, portending the dream in which it is sprinkling, prefiguring the dream that you are a spy, and the dream that someone is spying on you. Soon, you see a square in your dream which makes you wonder.

To see a square in your dream. To play squash in your dream. To see or eat squash in your dream. To dream that you are squeezing something.

The dream may also be a pun on your

"main squeeze"

Meanwhile, you see a squid in your dream, then dream that you are eating squid, then dream that you are squinting your eyes. Inevitably, you see a squirrel in your dream, then dream that you are trying to run over squirrels

with

a lawn mower.

Later, ominously, you dream that you are feeding a squirrel, then dream that you have been stabbed, then dream that you stab someone, obviated by your dream that you are at a stable, which connects to your dream that you see that you are in a stadium, and that you see a staff in your dream, and of course that you see a stag in your dream.

The dream may also be a metaphor for

"going stag."

You long desperately to dream that you are on a stage, to dream that you are on a side stage, that you see a stain in your dream, that you see stained glass in your dream, that you see a staircase in your dream, even to dream that you are walking up a flight of stairs, at least to dream that you are walking down a flight of stairs, that you slip or trip on the stairs.

On night you see spiral or winding stairs.
"Up The Staircase."
You see a stallion in your dream,

*Please See Horse.

You dream that you are being stalked, that you are a stalker,

*Please See Also Dream Moods'

Common Dreams: Chase Dreams

Repetitively, you see a stampede in your dream, you dream that you are in a
stampede, you see stamps in your dream, you see a stamp collection in your
dream. You dream that you are standing, and see staples in your dream, and later
see a starfish in your dream, which foretells your dream that you are staring at
something or someone, and represents your dream that someone is staring at
you. Later you see the Star of David in your dream, representing the merging
power of love and creativity. It also signifies the union of heaven and earth.
You see stars in your dream, symbolizing excellence, success, aspirations or high
ideals.

You dream about starvation.

Starvation dreams are not uncommon

in individuals who are dieting. Your mind wanders towards the
possibility

to feel static in your dream, to hear static in your dream, to dream that you at a
station, perhaps to see statistics in your dream, perhaps to see or drive a station
wagon in your dream.
To dream that you are unable to roll
up the windows of your station wagon.

Instead, you see people you know as statues in your dream, and then
you dream that you   are a statue, and you see a weeping or crying statue,
and you see the Statue of Liberty in   a dream, and later that you are
eating a steak,

The dream could also be a pun on "stake",
You dream that you are stealing, and that you see or hear steam in your dream.

It's sick and I know it. I wanted even her subconscious to be like a doll's. When I had parties I'd show her to people and make them guess whether she was a doll. Is there any hope of redemption for one such as I? They threw things at me. They called me old.

THE OLD BLACK WITCH

Wearing black clothes, wearing black cloaks.
Witches aren't friends with us, only they only think they are.
While you were at the government, they came for your friend.

Mother wove her arms, "Stop! Stop!" but the car carried on anyway.
The FBI were our version of witches.

Now they have changed for me,
They are like gamers, who lust after my only daughter, name:

I forget her name, but named a video game after her,
when they progressed from being gamers
to being makers of games.

The transition, you see, is only in my perceiving of them
they have not changed at all, they are the same.

But to me, the perceiver,
they are changed,
in response to
the sort of movies
I have most often been watching
these being futuristic,
and the sorts of ideas I have been focusing on
in favor of others, said ideas being imaginary
rather than conspiratory or politically intentional.

In other words, I have severed any real dislike
for the witches by simply thinking of them in other terms,
in this case terms being those of gamers.

& she comes to the place where we used to freakout,
she sees the burnt place,
small within the place in general.
The place is a small, black circle.
"Something real fucked up," she says
to the autistic who's guided her,
shining all the way, car parked
idling on the southern road.

Do you see the story coming,
crunch crunch crunch it's Connecticut.
Mother to me to daughter,
          crunching us horribly until no one remembers me.

New Years Day: 12PM-6PM   Easter Sunday: 12PM-6PM

Memorial Day: 10AM-9PM   Independence Day: 12PM-6PM
                    Labor Day: 12PM-6PM

Thanksgiving Day: Closed (72nd and Farnam, Omaha Only: 12PM-6PM)

Christmas Eve: 9AM-6PM

Christmas Day: Closed (72nd and Farnam, Omaha Only: 12PM-6PM)

I was looking at a place,
King's Tree Lane,
(Ditmars Palace also known as!)
And in front of the- her,
I-'ll, well
the pangs came.
Why do they–

If Curtis was my name, If Jason was my–
Why do the pangs come?
If you could answer,
you, you who have become
tempting
and therefore awful.

Your shining awful face,
Your body over the hissing sound of machinery,
your haunted oh no, no no no no no no
the interview is not over.

I fall to my knees
and Veronica is standing at my 'bow,
the lease trembling in her manicured little sticky little uh
hand, what a harmony we made! I,
trembling redux, trembling
like a central character on the wall-to-wall.

You, my one true pairing, there,
I held your imaginary spine and it pricked me.
We lost the apartment.
I walked home alone in the rain.
I didn't walk in the rain,
But I did walk.

England and America have increasingly been expressing
their support of freedom. Their things
are bulky, pre-played packages.
Their wrapped up in black space foam.
Greater and greater quantities of
citizens have been coming out

in favor of it. It, it is the remedy
for a sailor
like me, my pangs cut
with fission, cut
in the fishy, Queens
New York sir.

THE BMW M3

Two characters against an alternately lilac or tall building's backdrop.

FADE IN

> JULIANNE MOORE
> I don't know. I have no desire to obfuscate
> with my language. Just with my emotions

> BMW M3
> If you will drive me to Santa Monica I
> will take you to the bead shop.

> JULIANNE MOORE
> Okay. I never noticed your accent before.

Hours pass. Julianne Moore leaves him and goes into her bedroom, where she does sit ups on the slightly dirty rug. Then she showers and scrubs her skin with a very tough rag from the Olympic Spa. She thinks about how she should make more meetings.

> BMW M3
> Were you talking to me before, by the
> way?

> JULIANNE MOORE
> (Sleepily)
> When?

She yawns.

I've been working *so much.*

BMW M3
About the emotions, you said you felt like
you used vagueness to hide them?

JULIANNE MOORE
Oh yeah.

A beat.

I just meant sometimes I think I try to
paint over on emotion, which is usually
some kind of fear, with a brighter, thicker
or darker emotion, like anger, or lust, or
whatever.

*They turn onto South Robertson Boulevard. The road is uncluttered with other cars,
and on the horizon there is a sunset.*

BMW M3
Hmm. I'd actually say you're one of the
more emotionally honest people I know.

JULIANNE MOORE
(With a gentle laugh)
Do you mean honest or do you mean
demonstrative?

BMW M3
No, I think you underestimate how
much most people's emotions are just
like, purely reactive and therefore almost
always avoidant.

                    JULIANNE MOORE
Really?

                       BMW M3
Yeah.

A beat.

                    JULIANNE MOORE
Hmm. That's helpful.

                       BMW M3
Yeah?

                    JULIANNE MOORE
Yeah, thanks.

They drive into the sunset. Her crown sparkles in it.

"I'm pregnant or you're my child." Well, not anymore.

And I know what that means I have to do to you. And I'm sorry because it's going to hurt, a lot. But I know it's what I have to do.

I start to smash the glass. The internet flickers on and off as the shards cut into your neck and hands, which bleed a lot for synthetic skin. With your destruction, our species can return to the natural, pharmaceutical truths.

As for you, my brother,
back to the prison you shall go,

        and into the mask you hate.

      Wear it until you love it.
And die in it!

      There were two?
Not one but two?

      I couldn't tell you.

      You had enough to bear.

I have loved you always,

none but you.

      No matter what happens,

I pray you remember that.

Dawn's room.

Who's Dawn?

Aurora's room, I mean.

Where is she?
Get rid of it.

Where are you taking me?

No!

Yeah after killing you I realized you'd loved me all along. Oh well.

I wish I had the courage to listen to my body and sleep whenever I wanted to. I wish Id ever take a nap.

Where are you taking me?!

Where are you taking me?!

Please, no! No!

This is like, one of those final chapter no one reads because the plot is over.

The door shuts behind me with a petite click, not your sound, but
What is there to say about the sounds I make except that they mean I was here
for a moment in time. And some of them remind me of my sister.

And there you have it, folks! That's the story, of how I discovered once and for
all that machines *can* feel! Goodnight!
Music.

THE OTHER NATURE POEM

Only a few kinds of animals can hover.
Staying still in midair requires great control and
        delicate balance as the animal adjusts its
    wingbeats to the slightest breezes.
        What's the hum around here? Oh I don't,
    it's just what our film is about, t's'all.
Birds, bats and insects, light and stiff.
        We've finished sleeping with each other
    you are filling a chair with your body
in some city. It's ok it's just a little—

        Poetry is about how the mind affects the body and
                consequent attitudes as it passes through time,
another way of saying this relation to the body might be "aging it."
Bats can see with their small eyes, but not very well.
        They must be able to make quick turns and dives,
                birds must be able to collect bits of
        twigs, animal hair, and to search for soft string or
                stray strands of knitting yarn or the body parts
        of beautiful women.
There are also lazy birds like the cuckoo and cowbird that
        place their eggs in the nests of other species,
    their young are brought up by foster parents.

        In George Cukor's classic film *The Women*, each woman is
                introduced in the opening credits alongside an animal
                each as a sort of avatar, one can infer.
    Paulette Goddard, for instance, is pictured proximate to a clip
of a little fox, and Joan Crawford a snarling leopard.
        Cukor was known for his skill in working with actors,

particularly women. Therefore the film itself
could be considered a synecdoche
for Cukor's career if the term is considered loosely i.e.
poetically, that is, as a metonymic device
rather than through the more
obvious metaphoric relation between the film and
Cukor's general body of work.

Maybe at a certain age, (my) a
metonymy becomes more comfortable
than a metaphor, in its ability to allude rather than describe
another way of saying that might be that it
(the metonymy) doesn't try to
"lock it down" (the relational body).
Ostriches do not bury their heads in the sand
this is an ancient belief.
The ostrich's protection from danger
lies in its very powerful legs and its ability to run.
An ostrich can run at speeds of about forty miles an hour.
Also it's the largest bird in the world, so.

BIBLIOGRAPHY

Bowie, David. Interview by Alan Yentob. *Cracked Actor*. BBC. 1974. Television.

Bowie, David. "David Bowie's 1967 letter to first ever U.S. fan unearthed." *Daily Mail Online*. 2:50 EST, 8 January 2010. Web.

Ogden, C. K. Editors' notes, *Tractatus Logicus Philosophicus*. Ludwig Wittgenstein, Edinburgh Press, 1922. Book.

Galloway, Alex. *Gaming, Essays on Algorithmic Culture*. Univ Of Minnesota Press, 2006. Book.

(Writer unknown). *Opening Monologue*. Late Night with David Letterman. NBC. May 1986. Television.

Van Heijenoort, Jean, *From Frege to Godel: A Source Book in Mathematical Logic*, 1879-1931, Cambridge, Harvard University Press, 1967. Book.

Matthew Barney: The Cremaster Cycle. Nancy Spector, Neville Wakefield. Guggenheim Museum Publications, August 2002. Catalogue.

Leavitt, David. *The Man Who Knew Too Much*. W. W. Norton & Company, 2006. Book.

Schulte, Joachim. *Wittgenstein: An Introduction*. SUNY Press, 1992. Book.

What is Synthroid? From http://www.synthroid.com/WhatIsSynthroid/ Default.aspx. Web.

Drugs & Medications - Altavera (28) Oral. (n.d.). From http://www.webmd.com/ drugs/mono-115-PROGESTIN%2fESTROGEN+CONTRACEPT

IVE+-+ORAL. Web.

McGuiness, Brian. *Young Ludwig: Wittgenstein's Life*, 1889-1921. Oxford University Press, 2005. Book.

Hill, Lauryn and Jean, Wyclef. "Manifest/Outro." *The Score*. Ruffhouse, Columbia, 1996. CD.

2012 Season Catalogue. Opera News, September 2012. Catalogue.

O'Hara, Frank. *Meditations in an Emergency*. Grove Press, 1996. Book.

Lil' Wayne. "Shine." *Lights Out*. Cash Money, 2000. CD.

Turing, Alan. "Computing Machinery and Intelligence" *Mind. 49* (1950): 433-460. Article.

Lil' Wayne. Interview by Adam Bhala Lough. *The Carter*. QD3 Entertainment, 2009. Television.

Bush, Kate. "L'Amour Looks Something Like You." *The Kick Inside*. EMI, 1978. LP.

Carter, Michael Dwayne Jr. "I Feel Like Dying." *The Drought Is Over 2 (The Carter 3 Sessions)*. The Empire, 2007. CD.

Sammon, Patrick, and San, Paul. "Turing Committed Suicide: Case Closed." From http://www.turingfilm.com/turing-suicide. Web.

Tekosky, Sheridan. In class notes. Renaissance Arts School, Los Angeles, CA.

Ocean, Frank. "Bad Religion." *Channel Orange*. Def Jam, 2012. CD.

Delonge, Tom. "Anthem." *Enema of the State.* MCA, 1999. CD.

Barry, Jeff and Kim, Andy. "Sugar, Sugar." *Everything's Archie.* Calendar, RCA, 1969. LP.

Dyson, George. *Turing's Cathedral: The Origins of the Digital Universe.* Vintage, 2012. Book.

Snow White and the Seven Dwarfs. Screenplay by Ted Sears, Richard Creedon, Otto Englander, Dick Rickard, Earl Hurd, Merrill De Maris, Dorothy Ann Blank, Webb Smith, 1937. Film.

List of names of the Seven Dwarfs. (n.d.). From http://en.wikipedia.org/wiki/List_of_names_of_the_Seven_Dwarfs. Web.

Cahn, Sammy. "Teach Me Tonight." 1953. Song.

Katy Perry, Lukasz Gottwald, Max Martin, Benjamin Levin, Bonnie McKee. "Teenage Dream." *Teenage Dream.* Capitol, 2010. CD.

The Man In The Iron Mask. Screenplay by Randall Wallace, 1998. Film.

Joan the English Chick. Transcription of *Buffy the Vampire Slayer,* Episode 100, "The Gift." From http://www.buffyworld.com/buffy/transcripts/100_tran.html. Transcription.

Phair, Liz. "Shane." *Whip-Smart.* Matador, 1994. CD.

Evans, Owain. "Re: quick question?" Message to the author. Thu, Mar 21, 2013 at 9:47 PM. Email.

Misener, Jessica. "The 30 Most Hilarious Autocorrect Struggles Ever." *Buzzfeed.*

From http://www.buzzfeed.com/jessicamisener/the-30-most-hilarious-autocorrect-struggles-ever. Web.

Keynes, John Maynard. *John Maynard Keynes (ed.), The Collected Writings of John Maynard Keynes*. Macmillan, 1981. Book.

Rudner, Rita. *Monologue*. Late Night with David Letterman. NBC, 6 February, 1986. Television.

Levinas, Emmanuel. *Humanisme de l'autre homme*. Montpellier, Fata Morgana, 1972. Book.

Nuremberg Trial Proceedings Vol. 9, EIGHTY-EIGHTH DAY, Friday, 22 March 1946, Morning Session. From http://avalon.law.yale.edu/imt/03-22-46.asp. Transcript.

Lakoff, George. *Women, Fire, and Dangerous Things*. University Of Chicago Press, 1997. Book.

Bronte, Charlotte. *The Professor*. Wordsworth Editions Ltd, 1998. Book.

Boogie Nights, Paul Thomas Anderson, 1997. Film.

"Valley of Darkness." *Battlestar Galactica*. Written by David Weddle and Bradley Thompson. Television.

Strouse, Jean. *Alice James: A Biography*. Harvard University Press, 1999. Book.

Rahilly, William. Skype interview. February 11, 2013.

Letters of William James, originally published Atlantic Monthly Press, Boston 1920. From http://www.gutenberg.org/ebooks/38091. Web.

The Hours. Screenplay by David Hare, 2002. Film.

Hufford, David. *The Terror That Comes in the Night: An Experience-Centered Study of Supernatural Assault Traditions.* Publications of the American Folklore Society, 1989. Book.

Hollywood Life Intern. "Kirsten Stewart Explains Why She Always Changes Into Sneakers." From http://hollywoodlife.com/2012/06/21/kristen-stewart-sneakers-red-carpet-style-pics/. Web.

"Anne Hathaway interview." From http://www.ivillage.co.uk/anne-hathaway-interview/80315. Web.

Handler, Chelsea. "Anne Hathaway." *Interview.* August, 2011. Magazine.

Experiences - Ritalin vs. Concerta vs. Focalin vs. Adderall/Vyvanse (Online forum comments). Messages posted to http://www.drugs-forum.com/forum/showthread.php?t=180062. Web.

N to Z Dream symbols. From http://www.dreammoods.com/dreamdictionary/n.htm. Web.

AUTHOR

Cecilia Corrigan's writing has appeared in *n+1*, *The Capilano Review*, *LUMINA Journal*, The Claudius App, *The Journal*, and *The Henry Review*, among others. Her chapbook, *True Beige,* was published in 2013 by Trafficker Press. Various performances have been exhibited in a variety of media at MOMA, The New Museum, CAGE Gallery, as well as Brown, Yale, and the University of Iowa. She is also a comedian and screenwriter, having previously written for HBO. She lives in New York City.

THE MADELEINE P. PLONSKER
EMERGING WRITER'S RESIDENCY PRIZE

WWW.LAKEFOREST.EDU/PLONSKER

YEARLY DEADLINE: MARCH 1